Passport

To Your National Parks® Companion Guide

North Atlantic Region

Help Us Keep This Guide Up to Date

Every effort has been made by the author and editors to make this guide as accurate and useful as possible. However, many things can change after a guide is published—trails are rerouted, regulations change, techniques evolve, and so on.

We would love to hear from you concerning your experiences with this guide and how you feel it could be improved and kept up to date. While we may not be able to respond to all comments and suggestions, we'll take them to heart, and we'll also make certain to share them with the author. Please send your comments and suggestions to the following address:

FalconGuides
Reader Response/Editorial Department
P.O. Box 480
Guilford, CT 06437

Or you may e-mail us at:

editorial@GlobePequot.com

Thanks for your input, and happy travels!

Passport

To Your National Parks® Companion Guide

North Atlantic Region

Your Complete Guide to Cancellation Stamp Collecting

Randi Minetor

GUILFORD, CONNECTICUT
HELENA, MONTANA

AN IMPRINT OF THE GLOBE PEQUOT PRESS

FALCONGUIDES®

Copyright © 2008 Randi Minetor

Falcon and FalconGuides are registered trademarks of Morris Book
Publishing, LLC.

Text design by Nancy Freeborn
Maps by Tim Kissel © Morris Book Publishing, LLC

Library of Congress Cataloging-in-Publication Data is available on file.

ISBN: 978-0-7627-4470-1

Printed in the United States of America
10 9 8 7 6 5 4 3 2 1

Contents

Massachusetts 37

New Hampshire 81

New York 83

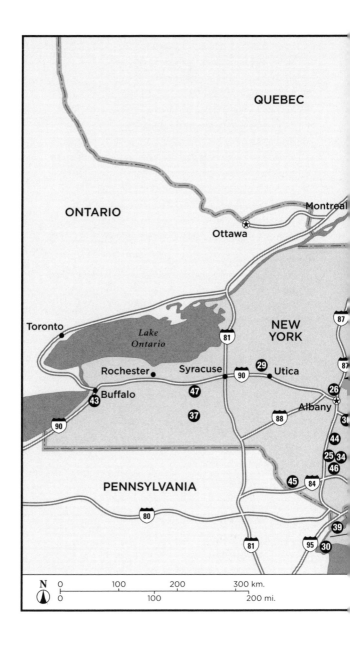

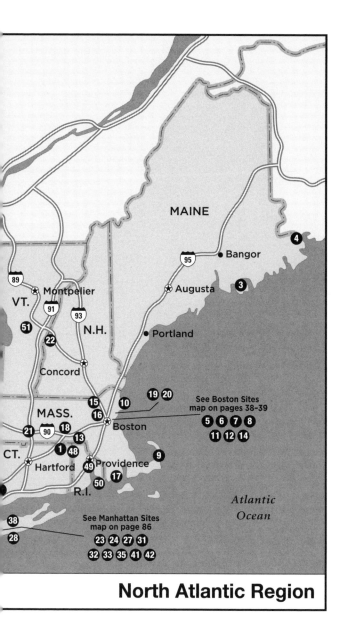

MAINE

95 • Bangor

4

89 ✪ Montpelier ✪ Augusta 3

VT. 91 93

51 N.H.

22 • Portland

Concord

15 10 19 20 See Boston Sites
MASS. 16 map on pages 38-39

21 90 18 Boston 5 6 7 8

13 11 12 14

1 48 9

CT. ✪ 49 Providence

Hartford 17

50

R.I. Atlantic
Ocean

38 See Manhattan Sites
map on page 86

28 23 24 27 31

32 33 35 41 42

North Atlantic Region

Preface

Friends and fellow Passport To Your National Parks® cancellation collectors have asked me why I took on the enormous project of creating a guidebook for my favorite hobby—an endeavor that has become a wonderful and endlessly fascinating part of my husband's and my life over the last seven years.

The need for this book hit me squarely between the eyes on a steamy August evening in 2002, when we stood in an empty Montana parking lot gazing at an inconspicuous green sign not 10 feet away that sealed our fate: PARK OPEN 8:30 A.M. TO 7:30 P.M. CENTRAL TIME.

Just across the state line in North Dakota stood the Fort Union Trading Post National Historic Site, our early evening destination, all rustic and inviting . . . and closed. Despite my calling ahead to check the closing time, despite the 90 miles of virtually empty road we'd traveled, and despite our fine planning . . . we had failed in our quest to collect our Passport cancellation.

Where had we gone wrong?

Nic and I had driven to North Dakota from our upstate New York home on an extended loop road trip that took the three of us—including June, my mother-in-law—to eleven official National Park sites across South and North Dakota, Montana, and Wyoming. For most people, such a trip through the scenic wonders of America's western prairie—the Badlands, the Black Hills, Wind and Jewel Caves, and the cataclysmic volcanic rupture that created Devils Tower—would be thrilling enough . . . but Nic and I traveled for a higher purpose. We were driven by our determination to collect Passport To Your

National Parks® cancellations at every park—and in some cases, to collect three, four, even five or more in one stop.

We'd hiked the rambling, wildflower-strewn quarry at Pipestone National Monument in Minnesota, descended more than 300 steps into the claustrophobic passageways of South Dakota's Wind Cave, and sat with thousands of spectators on benches in the late evening half-light to see Mount Rushmore's faces cast into shadows. We'd imagined Richard Dreyfuss's famed *Close Encounters of the Third Kind* mashed-potato sculpture of Devils Tower while standing at the base of its real-life counterpart, and we'd listened, enraptured, as a National Park Ranger revealed the irony in General Custer's ill-conceived battle at Little Bighorn. At every stop, we began our visit at the park bookstore, where we stamped our Passport book to commemorate the day. We came to get the cancellation, but we stayed because of the wonders we found.

Now in the home stretch, we had swooped down to the North Unit of Theodore Roosevelt National Park to get the Passport cancellation before the visitor center closed at 4:30 P.M., then made the drive back through the grasslands to Fort Union. On the way, I pulled out my mobile phone and called Fort Union to double-check the closing time. "Seven-thirty P.M.," the ranger confirmed. Not for one moment would it have occurred to me to respond with another question: "In which time zone?"

A funny thing happens to the time zone line in North Dakota. It zigzags along the edges of a dozen counties and through the middle of several, making the correct time a mystery to any unsuspecting traveler. Roughly following the path of the Missouri River, the time zone line even confuses some residents, who set their clocks to central time even though their neighborhoods are officially in mountain time.

So there was no way for us to know that in the top northwestern corner of the state, the time zone line veers sharply west, then follows the state border straight up to Canada.

We cruised up the long drive to the fort itself, enjoying the light of early evening as it turned the prairie the color of maple syrup. Then all three of us gasped at once. A tiny sign read: PARK OPEN 8:30 A.M. TO 7:30 P.M. CENTRAL TIME.

We looked at our watches. It was 6:45 P.M. mountain time . . . 7:45 P.M. central time.

Normal, sane travelers who had not been bitten by the Passport To Your National Parks® bug would have shrugged and driven away, skipping the fort altogether or leaving it for another vacation. We, however, schlepped back to Fort Union two days later to collect our cancellation, while Nic's mom sat in the back seat, counted yellow-headed blackbirds in the open fields, and chuckled at our misguided quest. The 97-mile back-track and hour-long visit to the fort—which turned out to be a charming fur-trading post with a droll mercenary perspective on the settlement of the Old West—set our trip back almost a full day.

On the return trip to Fort Union, Nic said casually, "If you're ever going to write another book, it should be a guide to the Passport program—so we never get stuck like this again."

This is that book.

The Passport program opens the door to magical moments and experiences you'll remember for a lifetime. With this book, you'll spend more time enjoying the parks and traveling to new places because you'll know exactly where to collect your Passport To Your National Parks® cancellations. I'm so pleased to have the opportunity to share this grand adventure with you and the hundreds of thousands of Passport cancellation collectors throughout the country. Enjoy your journey. Perhaps, on some distant mountain, in the recesses of a subterranean cavern, or in a visitor center in the nation's heartland, we'll meet and share our stories. I'll look forward to seeing all of your cancellations!

Acknowledgments

No project of this magnitude can come together unless many hands and minds join to make it happen—and I have literally hundreds of people to thank for their roles in bringing these field guides to bookshelves across America. In this limited space, I will acknowledge just a few of these helpful, encouraging, and supportive individuals.

First, I cannot say enough about the patient and persevering Scott Adams, executive editor for The Globe Pequot Press, the production team at Globe Pequot including the amazing Tracy Salcedo-Chourré and Shelley Wolf, and my extraordinary agent, Regina Ryan, for supporting this project from the beginning and seeing it through many channels and challenges over many months to bring about its eventual birth. Likewise, I thank Jason Scarpello and Chesley Moroz of Eastern National for their willingness to participate in this next extension of the Passport To Your National Parks® program. Rachel Shumsky and, later, Eileen Cleary at Eastern National maintained the list of Passport cancellation stamps at Eastern National's retail Web site, www.eparks.com, and they were quick to provide additional information when I needed it.

Many fellow Passport cancellation collectors were generous with their time and knowledge as I tackled the daunting task of pinpointing locations for every known, documented, and active cancellation in the country. Nancy Bandley's amazing National Park Travelers Club Master List was a tremendous tool, and I thank her for the use of this excellent information source. I am particularly grateful to my Internet friend John D. Giorgis, whose encyclopedic knowledge of the national parks system and his own adventurous travel tales were of great help—I do hope that John succeeds in his dream of becoming Secretary of the Interior one day. Dan Elias, Charlie and Rett Davenport-Raspberry, Greg Parkes, and Coleen Tighe all offered information and assistance, and I can't thank them enough for their insights.

Hundreds of national park and national heritage area rangers, staff members, supervisors, and volunteers answered my questions and took the time to return my calls, find facts, track down old cancellations, and verify new ones for me, often providing new kernels of information about their sites and the activities and lessons available at each. My respect for the National Park Service grew with each passing day as I connected with these well informed, gracious, and helpful people across the country. I thank all of them for their guidance, assistance, comments, and recommendations about the Passport program, as well as for their unfailing cheerfulness.

Here at home, I would be struggling through the final fact-checking to this day if not for my devoted and uncomplaining assistant, Dan O'Donnell, who followed up with every park and property and checked every cancellation's availability. To Martin Winer, my "writing date" buddy and lifelong friend, I am grateful for the long afternoons we passed with laptops and java in coffeehouses and sandwich shops throughout Rochester while each of us worked on our separate projects. There is nothing better than a friend who knows when to talk and when to just let be.

Finally, to my husband, Nic, the love of my life and the man who opened up this world of travel for me by sharing his passion for the two-lane blacktop, and then by discovering the Passport program and launching our own cancellation quest ... may our travels be long, may the wind be at our backs, and may we never run out of open roads to drive, nor days in which to drive them.

Introduction

Passport Stampers, Start Your Engines!

So you've crisscrossed the United States by car, plane, train, and bus, you've traversed scenic rivers by powerboat, airboat, kayak, and canoe, you've hiked rolling foothills, climbed summits, and gazed down into massive canyons. You've stood at the top of Yosemite National Park's Sentinel Dome, trekked across the fire-hot sands of Death Valley, canoed the rushing Middle Delaware River, and camped among the alligators in the Everglades. You've visited every major Civil War battlefield and every president's mansion, and you've seen every bed in which George Washington once slept.

That's all great, but did you get the Passport cancellation?

The coveted Passport cancellation—the symbol of the Passport To Your National Parks® program—has moved from its humble beginning as a souvenir of happy National Park travelers to become a goal in itself. Today more than 1.3 million families own the little blue book that has developed into a national pastime, and more than 75,000 of these books sell in National Park bookstores every year.

If you're a Passport owner, you know what I know: Passport cancellation collecting is no casual matter. Chances are you've planned at least one vacation with the goal of visiting the most national park sites in a single day or week, stopping at each visitor center to stamp your Passport book with the 1¼-inch-wide, dated cancellation that proves you were there.

The Passport To Your National Parks® is a breast-pocket-sized book that contains instructions for its use, basic maps of each of its nine regions, and blank pages for the collection of rubber stamp cancellations and for sets of colorful, adhesive-

backed stamps issued on an annual basis. Collectors will stop
at Passport cancellation stations in whatever national park they
visit and imprint their Passport books with the rubber stamp
cancellation they find there. Each cancellation has an adjust-
able date, so it is a permanent reminder of the very day the
Passport holder visited the park.

Cancellations record the date of your visit.

While the National Park Service currently divides the nation
into seven geographic regions, the Passport program recog-
nizes nine regional divisions to achieve an even distribution of
parks over all of the service's geographic regions. Regions are
designated in the Passport book by color, and each region
includes a color-block map of included states, a list of the
parks in that region, and blank pages for collection of *two* kinds
of stamps: the *rubber stamp cancellations* showcased in this
guide and *full-color, self-adhesive stamps* that are part of the
Passport To Your National Parks® Annual Stamp Series.

The color-coding extends to the cancellations themselves:
Cancellation stamps at each national park have ink colors that
coincide with their regional divisions. In other words, a cancel-
lation in Pennsylvania will have light blue ink to match the Mid-
Atlantic Region's designated color in the Passport book, a
Maine cancellation will have golden brown ink to match the
North Atlantic Region's color, and so on.

It may also be interesting to note that some cancellations
are expressed in a combination of upper case and lower case
type; others are typeset in all capital letters.

A note on the Annual Stamp Series: The self-adhesive sets, issued every spring, include ten full-color stamps. One park from each of the nine regions is showcased on a separate stamp with a photograph and brief description; each set also includes a larger National Stamp honoring a park that's celebrating a special anniversary or milestone in that year. Like the cancellations, the self-adhesive stamps each have a color bar that matches the region's color, making them very easy to place on the correct pages in the Passport book. The stamp sets—including those issued in previous years—are readily available at the parks and on the Internet at www.eparks.com. *Because the stamp sets are so easy to obtain, they are not the focus of this Passport program companion guide. Instead, I focus on the cancellations, which must be secured at the various sites themselves.*

In 2006, the twentieth anniversary of the Passport program was recognized with the introduction of the Passport To Your National Parks® Explorer, a deluxe Passport package that provides more detailed maps, more stamping pages, a ring binder that allows users to insert and remove pages, a water-resistant, zipper-closed outer cover, pockets for maps, brochures, and personal items, a pen, and a handy carrying strap. The Passport To Your National Parks® companion guides are the right size to slip into the Explorer's inside pocket.

You may choose to chase every Passport cancellation in every park or affiliate, including the many duplicate cancellations scattered through far-flung visitor centers and other cancellation stations, or you may prefer to collect just one cancellation from each park as you happen across it. You also may want to collect "bonus cancellations," unofficial cancellations of every shape, size, color, and form, found in hundreds of national parks as well as in incalculable numbers of unrelated sites in every state (more on these below).

So successful is this program that there are now more than 1,500 cancellations available in 391 national parks and in dozens of National Park Service affiliates! This guide will tell you exactly where to find them, extending the pleasure of your travel experiences by taking you into areas you might never discover on your own. You'll see more of each park, you'll gain a better understanding of why the U.S. Department of the Interior preserves these natural, historic, and cultural places, and you'll come home with a sense of accomplishment and a burning desire to hit the road again as soon as possible...because there are more cancellations out there, more places to see, and more two-lane blacktop roads to conquer.

A (Very) Brief History of Passport To Your National Parks®

In 1986, the National Park Service entered into a joint agreement with Eastern National, the organization that owns and manages the bookstores in most of the national parks east of the Mississippi River. The idea was simple: Create a program that provides visitors to the national parks with a free memento and invites them to increase the frequency and quantity of their national park visits by encouraging them to collect Passport cancellations.

The Passport To Your National Parks® program began with just one cancellation at each park, but as it grew, so did the number of cancellations offered at many of the larger parks. Over the course of years, parks began to order additional cancellations. Participation in the program has always been voluntary, but no park has rejected the program (with the exception of Hohokam Pima National Monument in Arizona, which is not open to the public). In fact, hundreds of sites have chosen to expand the potential for Passport stamping within their boundaries. The smallest parks may have just one cancellation on the property, but the more expansive parks—Great Smoky Mountains, Yellowstone, Grand Canyon, Acadia, Olympic, Everglades, Delaware Water Gap, and many others—offer anywhere from five to seventeen cancellations in bookstores, visitor centers, museums, train depots, ranger stations, lighthouses, and information kiosks, luring collectors to stray from the main paths and discover the hidden treasures beyond.

This guide will help you find the cancellations that you want to collect, while bringing others to your attention that you might never find on your own. Collect the ones that interest you, ignore the rest, and enjoy the Passport program in the way that suits your lifestyle, your budget, and your enthusiasm.

Duplicate Versus Unique: Which Cancellations You'll Find in the Parks

As of this writing, more than 1,500 official Passport To Your National Parks® cancellations are documented throughout the 391 National Park Service sites, affiliated areas, and heritage corridors.

Many parks place duplicate cancellations at visitor centers and other sites throughout their units, providing easy access for collectors who may only make one stop within the park. For example, Acadia National Park in Maine offers a generic cancellation at every visitor center throughout the park, for a total of six duplicates.

Meanwhile, at the same park, there are twelve cancellations with location-specific text, providing collectors with unique cancellations for Blackwood Campground, Schoodic Peninsula, Isle au Haut, Seawall Campground, Islesford, Jordan Pond, and others.

A generic, duplicate cancellation and a unique, place-specific cancellation.

Some Passport stampers collect all the duplicates as well as the unique cancellations they find in their travels. The idea of collecting an imprint from every Passport cancellation in the country appeals to some hard-core stampers, and they will return to parks again and again when new cancellations are added, even if they are identical to the originals.

Other collectors will skip the duplicates, collecting only the unique cancellations they find in each park. Each method provides its own rewards: Duplicate cancellation collecting will fill a Passport book quickly with places and dates, while collecting only the unique cancellations may save time on the road that would otherwise be spent chasing down duplicates.

In each park's entry, I note unique cancellations and duplicates to help you determine what you'd like to collect in the time you have. Cancellations that exist in only one location, with no duplicates, are noted in this guide as "unique" with a special **❶** icon. These are the most precious cancellations to most Passport cancellation collectors, as each is available at only one place in the entire country. Knowing which cancellations are unique will help you plan your travels for maximum collecting. Those cancellations that can be collected in any number of locations are noted in this book as "duplicate" with a corresponding **❶** icon.

Bonus Cancellations

In addition to the official cancellations, many Passport stampers collect the irregular "bonus" cancellation stamps they come across in their travels.

Bonus cancellations can come in any shape, size, or form. Some parks have a series of bonus cancellations in animal shapes, while others provide a commemorative cancellation to celebrate an important anniversary or milestone. Some are complex, depicting an entire landscape, scene, or architectural detail, while still others are simply larger and square instead of the regulation size and circular shape.

Travelers find these additional cancellations within and beyond the perimeters of the national parks: in the bookstores or offices of state-owned parks and historic sites, at presidential libraries, or at privately owned attractions. The rampant success of the Passport program certainly would encourage sites that are not part of this or any other stamping program to join in the fun.

A complete list of these odd and often transitory bonus cancellations would make this book too unwieldy to carry on stamping trips, but if you would like a list of all the bonus cancellations documented to date, visit www.parkstamps.org (the National Park Travelers Club Web site) and click on Master List.

About Changed and Missing Cancellations and Where to Send Updates

The Passport To Your National Parks® companion series endeavors to bring you the most accurate information possible about where to find Passport cancellation stamps in all National Park Service sites and affiliates.

Because the Passport program includes so many participating sites, changes can take place in the program without the knowledge of The Globe Pequot Press or this author. Cancellations sometimes wear out, become too damaged to use, are misplaced, or disappear entirely in the hands of selfish souvenir hounds. In addition, the increase in volunteers at national park sites, caused in part by recent budget constraints, means that many frontline information desk and visitor center assistants are not familiar with the Passport program.

Cancellations are often reordered, and staff members do not always order identical cancellations to those that have been lost or damaged. You are virtually certain to encounter occasional variations in spelling, punctuation, use of contractions, and actual wording on cancellations when compared to the cancellations listed in these guides. The original cancellation may be long gone or forgotten. You may hope that it is lingering in a desk drawer, waiting for an intrepid collector to inquire about it . . . but in reality, the chances of this are slim.

If you find that the cancellation you've collected at any site is not the one you expected, please contact me at foundstamp@minetor.com. I will make note of the change, post it on my official Web site at www.minetor.com/travel books, and pass the change on to the National Park Travelers Club for updating on the club's Master List. If you can e-mail a jpeg scan of your cancellation and include the exact location in which you found it, as well as your name, you will receive acknowledgement for your efforts on www.minetor.com/travelbooks.

Please do not harass rangers or any other park staff member or volunteer about missing cancellations. If you've inquired and the cancellation is not available, it's time to move on to your next stop, or to take some time to enjoy the park, visitor center, contact station, or historic site and its surroundings.

Needless to say, if you're traveling to a particularly out-of-the-way stamping location, call before you drive to be sure the cancellation is available.

Some Rules for Collecting Cancellations

The first and most important rule of Passport cancellation collecting is to enjoy the parks, whether you visit for an hour, a day, a week, or an entire season. We collect Passport cancellations because we love the parks in which they are found. Walk, bike, swim, paddle, explore, and learn as you travel.

Perhaps it's not necessary to say this, but Rule #2 is to show respect for the parks. The old adage, "Take nothing but pictures, leave nothing but footprints," holds true every day, and Passport stampers are leaders in demonstrating their commitment to park preservation. Leave artifacts or natural resources where you find them, pack out your own litter and that of others, and do no harm to the landscapes you came to admire.

About "Stamp and Run"

Here comes the collector, Passport book in hand, dashing to the cancellation station a few minutes before closing. He grabs the cancellation stamp, flips pages, bangs the stamp down onto the ink pad and smacks a quick imprint into his book... then rushes out again, with hardly a word of greeting to the staff member, ignoring the educational displays and the items for sale in the bookstore.

The dreaded "stamp and run" is the fastest way to meet the angry side of a park ranger—both because of the stamper's obvious disinterest in the park itself, and because the stamp-and-run perpetrator can appear indifferent, unfriendly, or downright rude. Passport cancellation seekers take heed: The ranger who is frustrated by your apparent lack of interest could be the same ranger who will come to your aid when you've strayed off the trail in the forest, or help you limp back to the visitor center when you turn an ankle on a rocky path.

If you must stamp and run, stop for a moment to explain the reasons for your abrupt behavior to the ranger or staffer behind the desk. Ask the ranger what's new at the park, and listen to the options for ways to extend your visit or plan a return trip. We all encounter days when nothing goes as planned, and we arrive at a park just in time to stamp the Passport before the visitor center shuts down for the night. But there still may be a pleasant twilight walk, an unexplored path, a previously overlooked historic structure, or a turnout with a wondrous view that we did not know existed until we asked.

Talk to Passport Fans Online

Thanks to the Web, Passport cancellation collectors from all over the country can connect and talk to one another, sharing lists of cancellations, secrets for obtaining record numbers of cancellations in single trips, and much, much more.

One of the best resources you'll find online is the Master List, a gargantuan Microsoft Excel document updated on a biweekly basis by Nancy Bandley. Known as the "Stamp Queen," Nancy boarded a seaplane with her husband, Dennis, and reached her 388th park—Aniakchak National Monument and Preserve in Alaska—in June 2005. This list not only catalogs all of the official cancellations, it also lists every bonus, or unofficial, cancellation discovered to date, as well as the lost, retired, or stolen cancellations that are no longer available.

You can find the list on a Web discussion board run by the National Park Travelers Club at www.parkstamps.org, one of several sites at which Passport cancellation collectors share anecdotes and discoveries from the road.

If a motorcycle is your preferred vehicle, check out the Iron Butt Association's National Park Service Motorcycle Touring forum at http://forums.delphiforums.com/NPSTouring/messages. These itinerant road warriors consider traveling from park to park an endurance sport. They know all the ins and outs of collecting, and their tips for safe, long-distance riding are invaluable to any cycle enthusiast.

How to Use This Book

This companion guide series is divided into nine books to match the regions in the Passport program. The states are listed alphabetically within each region, and the parks are alphabetized within each state.

In addition to the 391 official national parks, you'll find national park affiliated areas and National Heritage Areas and Corridors listed within each state. Virtually all of these affiliates have Passport cancellations, although participation in the Passport program is spottier because the sites are less centralized. Management of affiliated areas and National Heritage Areas and Corridors is in the hands of state and local agencies rather than the National Park Service. Some are exquisitely managed and maintained—the Oklahoma City National Memorial is a standout in this regard—while others are spread out across a wide geographic area, making it more difficult for management to keep tabs on the location and maintenance of Passport cancellations.

Here's what you'll find on each page of this guide:

- The official National Park Service name and designation for the park.

- The state and town or city in which the park is located (or where the park's headquarters is located for multilocation parks).

- The park's main information telephone number and Web address—you'll need these to double check park hours, to make certain that the park is actually open on the day you want to go there, and to plan the activities you'd like to enjoy during your visit. Even though park hours are provided in this book, anything from bad weather to budget shortages can close a visitor center or outlying building without notice.

- The park's time zone. In this guide, all parks are within the eastern time zone, so this entry has been omitted.
- Total number of cancellations at each park, with additional totals for cancellations for other sites you may find at these stops.
- The degree of difficulty in obtaining the park's Passport cancellations. Every park has a rating of **Easy, Tricky, Challenging,** or **Heroic,** helping you understand the hurdles you must vault to collect all of the cancellations in each park.

Easy: The park is open 362 days or more each year and has only one or two cancellations, which are readily accessible at the bookstore or visitor center. Essentially, if you show up during business hours any day but Thanksgiving, Christmas, or New Year's Day, the cancellation is yours.

Tricky: Something's up at this park, and you'll need to be alert to get the cancellation. The park is open only during limited hours or on an erratic or seasonal schedule. There's more than one cancellation, and there's an obstacle—the cancellation stamp is hidden in a desk drawer, a long-closed visitor center waiting for repairs, a task that must be performed before the cancellation can be obtained. Look for the "Stamping tips" to find out what's going on.

Challenging: There are lots of cancellations in this park, and it may take more than one day to get them all and still enjoy what this park has to offer. Cancellation collecting may require an unusual physical effort, like a long walk (more than a mile) to the stamping site, or the many units involved are open on a limited basis. You'll go well out of your way to finish stamping in this park. The "Stamping tips" will help you figure out what to do—and for the parks with the most cancellations, there's a suggested route for maximum stamping success.

Heroic: Slap on that seasickness patch and strap in! You'll need to endure a long ferry ride—or two—on choppy water, charter a seaplane, or jet out to an exotic island to get this one. There may be only one cancellation at each of these parks, but it will be hard-won, and you'll be talking about this trip for years to come.

- A short description of the park and why it exists, providing baseline information about what you can see, do, or learn when you go.

- "Stamping tips," with cautions, twists, and turns encountered by some of the most well traveled Passport participants in the country.

- "Don't miss this!" takes you beyond the brochure to find the gems in each park—sights, sounds, and activities you might not discover on your own. "Don't miss this!" is highlighted with an 🛈 icon.

- Park hours and fees are broken down by individual visitor center or other cancellation stamp location.

- Driving directions to the sites from the nearest major highways or cities.

- Stamping locations and what the cancellations say is the meat-and-potatoes for each park. The cancellation's specific location, any pertinent information on that location, and the cancellation's exact text are provided in this section. The text on each cancellation is listed uniformly to help you determine if you have found the correct cancellation. The text that arches around the top half of the cancellation is listed first. A "/" (forward slash) signals the end of the top text, and the text following the "/" fills the bottom half of the cancellation. *The text is listed exactly as it appears on the cancellation: If it's listed in this guide in all capital letters, then the cancellation itself was made that way. Occasionally a misspelling appears on a cancellation; these are not corrected in this guide, but presented as they appear.*

Unique cancellations are identified with a ❶. These cancellations have no duplicates. There's only one place to find each of these, so you'll want to build stops for these cancellations into your travel plans.

Duplicated cancellations are identified with a ❿. These cancellations can be found in more than one place.

While we believe that all the existing cancellations have been cataloged here, you may come across new or hitherto undetected official Passport cancellation stamps that are not in this book. If so, we want to hear from you! Please send any updates to me at foundstamp@minetor.com. Include the text of the cancellation, the place you found it, and as much detail as possible about where this cancellation resides. If possible, send a jpeg scan of the cancellation. I'll post updates at my Web site for this purpose, www.minetor.com/travelbooks.

In addition to this book and your official Passport, you need one more thing: America the Beautiful—The National Parks and Federal Recreational Lands Pass. This pass will provide you and the other passengers in your single-family vehicle (or your spouse, parents, and children) with free or discounted admission for one year to every park site in the system, as well as other sites managed by the federal government. You'll find that your pass will pay for itself in one trip. Purchase your pass from the National Parks Foundation at www.nationalparks.org, or at any national park site.

Buckle up—it's time to hit the road.

The North Atlantic Region

The sheer number of pivotal events in American history that took place in the North Atlantic Region—from the "shot heard 'round the world" to the launching of the women's suffrage movement—would be enough reason to make a good, long visit to New York and the six New England states and immerse yourself in an era that crackled with drama. The streets of Boston, the hills of Saratoga, the lush countryside of the Finger Lakes, and the streets of Rhode Island all contain tales that reveal the origins of the freedoms we have the luxury of taking for granted today. This corner of America produced long lists of heroic names that are still spoken in every household in the nation, and their deeds are immortalized in song and poem.

The battles of the American Revolution are the first things we think of when we consider these states, but history unfolded here in dozens of significant ways. Industry's inventions became the tools that turned raw materials into mass-produced finished products along the Atlantic coastline, from forged iron in Saugus, Massachusetts, to guns at Springfield Armory in the same state, while the treasures of the sea found their way to American homes and tables through New Bedford and Salem. The Erie Canal transported all of these materials inland from the Hudson River, strengthening New York state and turning it into a commercial center, while mansions sprang up along the Hudson and turned Hyde Park into one of the nation's most prestigious residential neighborhoods.

What draws people to the North Atlantic Region, however, goes well beyond history. The legendary Atlantic coastline, with mountains that rise from the sea's edges and long, gracious miles of empty beaches and wind-chiseled dunes, provides recreational and renewal opportunities from the northern tip of Maine to the islands off New York City. Whether you beach-comb in the summer, leaf-peep in the fall, or cross-country ski the snow-crusted paths in winter, you'll find visual pleasure as far as you can see, even in the shadow of the nation's most populated city.

To maximize the pleasure of your visit to the North Atlantic Region, here are some basic guidelines:

- Don't drive in New York City or Boston. These congested cities are jammed with motorists at any hour, and parking can be prohibitively expensive or entirely unavailable. The good news is that both cities have excellent public transportation in safe, clean vehicles. You needn't fear the New York sub-way system if you have a good map and you pay attention to the passing stops until you reach your own. Visit www.mta .nyc.ny.us for maps of the New York subway and bus routes, and www.mbta.com for Boston's famous trains.

- Watch the weather. This is snow country, so if you're traveling in winter or early spring, pay close attention to weather reports and the radar. In upstate New York in particular, the Great Lakes create their own storms with "lake effect snow," a phenomenon that can white out the New York State Thruway with bands of sideways-falling precipitation with virtually no advance warning. Maine is known for its "nor'easter" storms, and snow can fall in the upper part of the state as early as late September. If you're not used to driving in this kind of weather, bring a good book and spend the day off the road in a warm, comfortable place.

- Remember that everything is fairly close together. One of the great things about cancellation stamp collecting in this region is that the parks are not far from one another, and some of the states themselves are the smallest in the country.

You'll find that the one national park site in Vermont, Marsh-Billings-Rockefeller National Historic Park, is just a twenty-minute drive from Saint-Gaudens National Historic Site, the only national park site in New Hampshire. It takes a little more than an hour to drive the entire length of Rhode Island, from the state line north of Providence to the seashore in Newport, leaving you plenty of time to tour the park sites there and continue on to eastern Connecticut to enjoy the picturesque Quinebaug & Shetucket Rivers Valley National Heritage Corridor. In Massachusetts, nearly all of the sites are centered in and around Boston, with some just north or south of the city, making it possible to enjoy this entire area over a period of two or three days without spending those days in the car.

Other National Park Service Affiliates and Areas

For your reference, the following National Park Service Affiliated Areas and National Heritage Areas in the region do not participate in the official Passport program:

- **Kate Mullaney National Historic Site, Albany, New York:** not yet open to the public.
- **Roosevelt Campobello National Historic Site:** This affiliate has a very attractive bonus cancellation, ordered so that the site could accommodate its cancellation stamp–collecting visitors. The site, located in Lubec, Maine, and Welshpool, New Brunswick, is comanaged by the U.S. and Canadian governments.
- **Hudson River Valley National Heritage Area, New York:** To date, no National Heritage Area–specific cancellation stamps have been ordered for this area, although you will travel through it when you visit historic sites including the Home of Franklin D. Roosevelt, Vanderbilt Mansion, and Eleanor Roosevelt National Historic Sites, and Thomas Cole House.

Three National Partnership Wild & Scenic Rivers in the North Atlantic Region did not have Passport cancellation stamps when this book went to press. They are listed here for reference:

- **Farmington National Wild & Scenic River, Connecticut**
- **Lamprey National Wild & Scenic River, New Hampshire**
- **Sudbury, Assabet, and Concord National Wild & Scenic Rivers, Massachusetts**

Just before this guide went to press, the Underground Railroad Network to Freedom added cancellations in this region. A dedicated entry on the network is not included, but cancellations are listed at the site in the book.

Amtrak Trails & Rails Program

A special Passport cancellation opportunity
www.nps.gov/trails&rails

Since the earliest days of the National Park Service, visits to the most remote and rugged parks often were accomplished by train—and it's this long association between national parks and train travel that led Amtrak and the National Park Service to create Trails & Rails, an unusual partnership that combines travel on the tracks with an opportunity to learn the natural and human history of the parks you pass along the way.

Here's how it works: When you buy a ticket on one of the participating trains and ride the train on one of the days the program is offered, you can take part in a lecture and question-and-answer session in the lounge car as you ride from one end of the train's route to the other. Led by well-versed volunteers, these programs provide in-depth information about one or more parks on the route...and at each program, Passport cancellation collectors can get a special cancellation that's only offered during these special Trails & Rails sessions.

It sounds simple enough to acquire these cancellations, but it's trickier than you think. Most of the Trails & Rails programs are offered from Memorial Day to Labor Day, and only on certain days of the week—and if a volunteer turns out not to be available, the program may be scuttled for that trip. The cancellations are kept in a traveling trunk that the volunteer picks up before boarding, so they don't actually "live" on the trains, and are not available on days when there is no Trails & Rails program.

Additionally, you need to ride the trains from a specific departure point and to a specific disembarkation point to be sure that a Trails & Rails program is scheduled on that train. For example, the Sunset Limited train runs from Orlando, Florida, to Los Angeles, California, but the two Trails & Rails programs offered on this train take place between Del Rio and Alpine, Texas (for Amistad National Recreation Area), and between New Orleans, Louisiana, and Houston, Texas (for Jean Lafitte National Historical Park & Preserve). You need to be on the train between these cities to have access to the cancellations, as the volunteer guides board in the first city and depart in the latter.

In the off-season, from Labor Day until Memorial Day, these train-specific cancellations may be kept at the participating parks, but it's also possible they will languish in the traveling trunk until the next Memorial Day. If you are determined to collect these cancellations, the sure-fire way to do so is to ride the trains on the right days.

You can research all of the opportunities and buy your tickets on the Amtrak Web site at www.amtrak.com.

- First, choose your route by clicking on "Routes" and choosing the name of the train from the pull-down menu.
- When the information about your train comes up, scroll to the bottom of the page for the "At A Glance" listing.
- Click on the name of the train. A pdf file of the train's current schedule will download to your computer.
- Open the pdf file and scan the document for the Trails & Rails listing, probably at the bottom of the last page, where "Services" are listed. This will tell you the days on which the Trails & Rails program is offered on this route.
- Make your reservations online by clicking on the "Reservations" tab at the top of the page, or call (800) USA–RAIL to talk with a reservations specialist, who can confirm that the Trails & Rails program will be offered on your travel date.

More information on the trains, participating parks, and routes is available at www.nps.gov/trails&rails.

Trails & Rails: North Atlantic Region

Two trains in the North Atlantic Region offer Amtrak Trails & Rails cancellations on three routes.

Adirondack
New York, New York, to Albany, New York
☐ Vanderbilt Mansion NHS/Adirondack **①**

Adirondack
Albany, New York, to Montreal, Quebec
☐ Saratoga Nat'l Historical Park/Adirondack **①**

Vermonter
Saint Albans, Vermont, to Springfield, Massachusetts
☐ Springfield Armory Nat'l Hist Site/Vermonter **①**

Connecticut

1 Quinebaug & Shetucket Rivers Valley National Heritage Corridor

Connecticut NPS Affiliated Area
Putnam, Connecticut
(860) 963–7226
www.nps.gov/qush

Number of cancellations: Two

Difficulty: Tricky

About this site: Is this truly the "last green valley" between Boston and Washington, D.C.? Surely the Quinebaug & Shetucket Rivers Valley is one of the most picturesque, remaining stubbornly rural while urban sprawl encroaches all around its 1,086 square miles (695,000 acres) in Connecticut and Massachusetts. Forests, farmlands, and villages form the nexus for a scant 300,000 residents who remain true to the small town culture that has existed here for centuries. In addition to the two rivers from which the corridor gets its name, this expansive valley holds more than eighty crystal-blue ponds and lakes, seven state forests, and sixteen state wildlife management areas.

Stamping tips: Obtaining cancellations for this corridor is historically tough. Despite advertised hours, the Prudence Crandall Museum suffers from funding issues that have forced its temporary closing on more than one occasion. Call before you visit.

A cancellation for the river corridor is also available in Massachusetts. See the Massachusetts chapter in this guide for details on collecting this cancellation.

❶ Don't miss this! Prepare for your trip by downloading maps from www.thelastgreenvalley.org, which will provide scenic routes and any number of shopping and restaurant recommendations. If you have more time, take a walk—climb Mount Misery, a 411-foot rise that offers a view all the way to Rhode Island, or walk the segment of the Charter Oak Greenway from Hampton to Pomfret, following a former railroad bed through the James L. Goodwin State Forest. This 11-mile segment of improved trail passes dry-laid stone walls, a beaver dam, innumerable opportunities to view wildlife, rushing streams, and, in spring, meadows in full bloom.

The Prudence Crandall Museum remembers the woman who founded the first school for young girls of color in 1833. Crandall originally opened her school for girls of wealthy families, but when she admitted an African-American student, her clientele quickly pulled away. Within a year, Crandall had shifted her original concept and regrouped, opening the school to young African American girls exclusively and maintaining her enrollment in the face of harsh discriminatory laws created specifically to force her to close. Crandall's story is one of many tucked into national park affiliated sites—stories of courageous women who broke new ground for equal rights in the face of restrictive, harshly prejudicial public policy.

Virtually any road you choose to drive in this corridor will provide the sort of lush landscapes and visual quietude you look for when you escape to the country, from the curved sweep of green and growing farmlands to exquisitely preserved, centuries-old homes. One of the most striking of these is the Samuel Huntington Homestead in Scotland, Connecticut—Huntington was a signer of the Declaration of Independence—which managed to avoid the ravaging many historic homes endured by remaining in private hands until 1994. The house is now both a museum and an archeological excavation site, as studies reveal that Native Americans lived on this land before Huntington family built their home in the 1730s.

Hours: The Prudence Crandall Museum is open Wednesday to Sunday, 10:00 A.M. to 4:30 P.M. It is closed December 15 through January 31.

The Lebanon Historical Society Museum is open Wednesday to Saturday, noon to 4:00 P.M.

Fees: The Prudence Crandall Museum charges $3.00 for adults, $2.00 for seniors and students six to seventeen, and is free for children under five.

The Lebanon Historical Society charges $3.00 for adults, $2.00 for children twelve to eighteen, and is free for children under twelve.

How to get there: Major access roads are Interstate 84 from Hartford and Interstate 395 from the New London area and Worcester. Within the heritage corridor, a 32-mile section of Connecticut 169 is a National Scenic Byway and a 19.5-mile section of Connecticut 49 is a state Scenic Byway.

Stamping Locations and What the Cancellations Say

Prudence Crandall Museum

At the junction of Connecticut 14 and CT 169 in Canterbury
(860) 546-9916

☐ Quinebaug-Shetucket NHC/Prudence Crandall Mus. ⓿

Lebanon Historical Society Museum

856 Trumbull Highway (Connecticut 87), Lebanon
(860) 642–6579

☐ Quinebaug-Shetucket NHC/Lebanon Hist. Soc. Mus. ⓿

2 Weir Farm National Historic Site

Wilton, Connecticut
(203) 834–1896
www.nps.gov/wefa

Number of cancellations: One

Difficulty: Tricky

About this site: In a different time, when art centered on nature scenes, and subjects and artists believed that they needed to separate themselves from the noise and grime of city life to produce great work, a new movement in uniquely American painting found a home here. J. Alden Weir, one of the nation's first American impressionist painters, purchased this farm and opened it to his counterparts as a center for artistic pursuit, painting many of his own greatest works based on the landscape and grounds he loved. Weir, Childe Hassam, John Twachtman, and others of a select group known as the Ten American Painters spent weeks and seasons on the site for thirty-seven years, until Weir's passing in 1919.

The legacy continued as Dorothy Weir took over her father's farm and studio and painted while her husband, sculptor Mahonri Young, created small bronzes and larger monuments in a studio he built on the grounds. When Mahonri passed away in 1957, the property was sold to locat artists Doris and Sperry Andrews. Today artists participate in an artist-in-residence program and continue to produce many remarkable works, both within and outside of the impressionist tradition.

Stamping Tips: Watch for irregular hours from November to April. Call before you drop in.

Don't miss this! To experience the inspiration that led Weir and his contemporaries to this pastoral place, walk the grounds and see the landscape through Weir's eyes. Pick up the Historic Painting Sites Trail Guide paintings in the visitor center and take the self-guided tour, stopping exactly where he placed his easel to view the blends of color and texture he captured on canvas. Or bring watercolors or oils and create a painting of your own, choosing from dozens of vistas that have moved artists for more than a century.

Hours: The grounds are open daily from dawn to dusk. From November through April, call for hours of operation. From May through October, the visitor center is open Wednesday to Sunday from 9:00 A.M. to 5:00 P.M. It is closed Thanksgiving, Christmas, and New Year's Day.

Fees: All facilities and tours are free.

How to get there: To reach the site from the north, take Interstate 84 south to exit 3 for U.S. Highway 7 in Danbury. Follow US 7 to the Branchville section of Ridgefield. Turn right (west) onto Connecticut 102 at a traffic light. Take the second left onto Old Branchville Road. Turn left at first stop sign onto Nod Hill Road. Follow Nod Hill Road 0.75 mile to the top of the hill. The parking lot is on the left and the visitor center is on the right at 735 Nod Hill Road.

From the south, take the Merritt Parkway/Connecticut 15 or Interstate 95 to US 7 northbound in Norwalk. Follow US 7 to the Branchville section of Ridgefield. Turn left (west) onto CT 102 at the traffic light, and follow the directions above to Weir Farm.

Stamping Locations and What the Cancellations Say
Weir Farm Visitor Center

☐ Weir Farm National Historic Site/Wilton-Ridgefield, Ct **❶**

Maine

3 Acadia National Park

Bar Harbor, Maine
(207) 288–3338
www.nps.gov/acad

Number of cancellations: Seventeen for Acadia, plus two cancellations for St. Croix Island International Historic Site

Difficulty: Challenging

About this site: The former playground of the very, very rich, Acadia's 47,000 protected acres span several islands that are the sheer definition of the rugged, sea-swept New England coast. Granite cliffs, mountains that appear to rise directly from the ocean's surface, and hillsides covered in evergreens are the part and parcel of Acadia's attraction.

But the real story of this park goes deeper than its scenery. Native peoples inhabited this land at least 5,000 years ago, and since then Acadia has served as a way point for European explorers and a home for early settlers, eventually attracting the region's most affluent residents, who built estates they called "cottages" on Mt. Desert Island. They left behind 45 miles of groomed carriage roads that offer some of the finest bicycling, hiking, and horseback riding opportunities in the national park system.

Stamping tips: There's no question that you'll need at least two days to collect all of Acadia's cancellations, even if you skip the duplicates—and that's without spending much quality time in this splendid park. You'll encounter plenty of obstacles to collecting here, especially if you travel to Acadia off-season—many of the park's facilities begin to close in mid-September, and by October 31, all have closed for the winter except for the Winter Visitor Center at the park headquarters.

The Hulls Cove Visitor Center opens on April 15, weather permitting, and extends its evening hours beginning June 15. The two cancellations at Hulls Cove Visitor Center are kept in a case behind the counter; you must ask for them. Many other facilities do not reopen until mid-June or even July.

Be sure to ask at park headquarters for the Saint Croix Island stamp. It's not kept in plain view and not everyone knows it's there. Be politely insistent about this one.

The greatest challenge to completing your Acadia cancellation collection in one day is the trip to Isle Au Haut, which requires a one-and-a-half hour drive from Bar Harbor to Stonington. Take Maine 3 north to Ellsworth, then turn left on Maine 172. Follow ME 172 to Maine 15, and continue on ME 15 south to Stonington. There, you'll board a ferry for a forty-minute ride to the Isle Au Haut town landing. The Isle Au Haut Boat Company sails from Stonington and docks about 1 mile from Acadia's unit on this island. One-way tickets are $16.00 for adults and $8.00 for children, and the ferry makes several round-trips daily. Call (207) 367–5193, or visit www.isleauhaut.com/schedule.htm, for a full schedule and to make reservations.

If you have a few days and you want to explore at a leisurely pace, you may choose to rely on public transportation. The Island Explorer shuttle buses are fare-free, and they travel to just about every stamping location on Mount Desert Island (except Cadillac Summit), and to the ferry terminals in Northeast and Southwest Harbors. Visit www.exploreacadia.com/maps.html for maps of the shuttle's eight routes and a complete schedule. One drawback: Generally, the routes do not overlap, so to transfer from one shuttle route to another, you may need to ride all the way back into Bar Harbor and change shuttles at the Village Green. One route from Hulls Cove Visitor Center goes directly to Park Loop Road; look for the Gold Route (number 4).

Don't miss this! You can drive up to the top of Cadillac Mountain to get your cancellation, but wouldn't you feel great about yourself if you hiked instead? At 1,530 feet, Cadillac is the highest peak in Acadia, but not so high that you'll need to adjust to the altitude—and the North Ridge Trail, considered a moderate hike with many level stretches, is a manageable two-hour walk, even if you include huffing-and-puffing breaks. Your pauses for breath are entirely justified as you drink in the sight of Frenchman Bay, deceptively smooth and tranquil from your newly achieved height.

For more challenge, choose the longer and more rugged South Ridge Trail, a 3.5-mile ascent through evergreen woods and over granite to the mountaintop. You've heard that Cadillac Mountain is the place where the sun rises first in the United States, and that's true—at least, from October 7 through March 6. Catch the fall colors and a glorious sunrise in an autumn trip to the top.

Acadia is famous for its carriage roads, 45 miles of wide, chipped-stone country paths that once yielded to the hooves of noble teams drawing the surreys of the very wealthy on their Sunday outings. The Astors, Rockefellers, Carnegies, and Vanderbilts all spent seasons here, and their resources kept these trails well groomed for their personal enjoyment. Today they are open to horseback riders, bicyclists, hikers, and joggers. Forbidden to motorized vehicles and tucked away from the Park Loop Road, these peaceful roads bring you just a little closer to the wilderness that often seems so distant in the Northeast, circling crystal blue lakes and meandering along forest edges where beech, maple, and birch trees provide shade. Rent a bike in Bar Harbor, and don't feel ashamed if the upward stretches force you to hop off and walk—even the roads rated as easiest feature rolling hills with long, slow inclines and precipitous descents.

Hours: Parts of Acadia National Park are open year-round, although most of the facilities and many of the roads are closed in winter. From December 1 to April 15, most of the Park Loop Road, including the road to Cadillac Mountain, is closed.

Hulls Cove Visitor Center is open April 15 through June, and in October, from 8:00 A.M. to 4:30 P.M. daily. In July and August, hours are 8:00 A.M. to 6:00 P.M. daily; in September, 8:00 A.M. to 4:30 P.M. daily. The visitor center is closed from November 1 to April 15.

Winter Visitor Center/Park Headquarters is open from November 1 to mid-April from 8:00 A.M. to 4:30 P.M. daily. It is closed Thanksgiving Day, Christmas Eve, Christmas Day, and New Year's Day. From mid-April to October 31, the center is open Monday to Friday, 8:00 A.M. to 4:30 P.M.

Islesford Historical Museum is open the third Monday in June through September daily from 9:00 A.M. to 3:30 P.M.; it opens at 10:45 A.M. on Sundays. It is closed daily from noon to 12:30 P.M. It is also closed October 1 through mid-June.

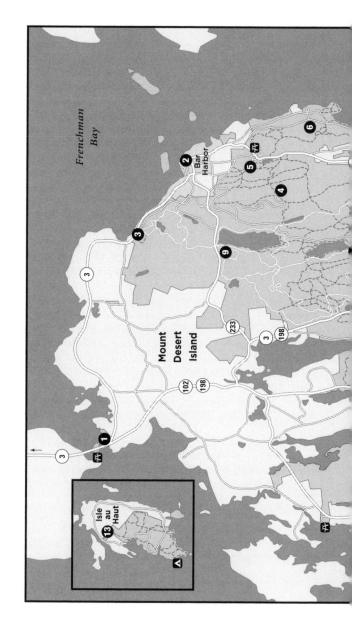

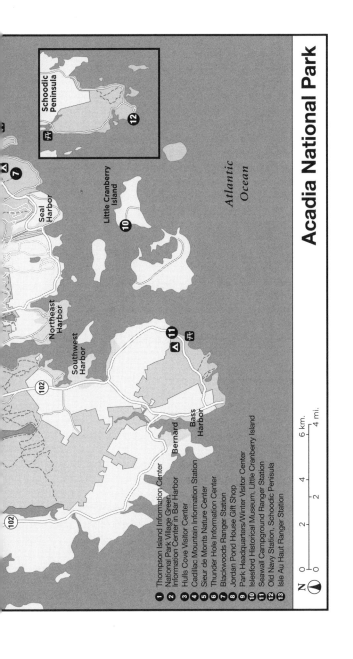

Acadia National Park

Schoodic Peninsula

12

Seal Harbor

7

Northeast Harbor

Little Cranberry Island

10

Southwest Harbor

11

Atlantic Ocean

102

Bernard

Bass Harbor

102

1. Thompson Island Information Center
2. National Park Village Green Information Center in Bar Harbor
3. Hulls Cove Visitor Center
4. Cadillac Mountain Information Station
5. Sieur de Monts Nature Center
6. Thunder Hole Information Center
7. Blackwoods Ranger Station
8. Jordan Pond House Gift Shop
9. Park Headquarters/Winter Visitor Center
10. Islesford Historical Museum, Little Cranberry Island
11. Seawall Campground Ranger Station
12. Old Navy Station, Schoodic Peninsula
13. Isle Au Haut Ranger Station

N

0   2   4   6 km.
0   2   4 mi.

Sieur de Monts Nature Center is open in June from 9:00 A.M. to 5:00 P.M. in July and August from 9:00 A.M. to 5:00 P.M.; and from September to mid-October from 9:00 A.M. to 4:00 P.M. It is closed mid-October through early May, and open on weekends only beginning in early May.

Thompson Island Information Center is open from mid-May to mid-September, 9:00 A.M. to 5:00 P.M. It is closed from mid-September to mid-May.

The ranger stations are generally staffed during the park's open hours. Rangers may be out in the field or otherwise unable to staff stations at all times, so cancellation stamp collecting can be hit and miss.

Fees: $20.00 per car for a seven-day entrance permit; $5.00 per individual pedestrian, motorcyclist, or bicyclist for a seven-day entrance permit.

How to get there: From Boston, take Interstate 95 north to Augusta, Maine. From Augusta, take Maine 3 east to Ellsworth and on to Mount Desert Island.

You can also take I–95 north to Bangor, Maine. From Bangor, take U.S. Highway 1A east to Ellsworth; from Ellsworth take ME 3 to Mount Desert Island.

Stamping Locations and What the Cancellations Say

The cancellations are listed in the order you will encounter them if you follow ME 3 from Bar Harbor to the park and around the Park Loop Road. Cancellations available off the loop road are listed at the end.

Thompson Island Information Center

Located on ME 3 as you cross from the mainland to Mount Desert Island

☐ Acadia National Park/Bar Harbor, ME **Ⓓ**

National Park Village Green Information Center

No direct phone line here; call (207) 288–3338 for information

Located in Bar Harbor on Firefly Lane, just off the Village Green, where the Island Explorer bus stops

☐ Acadia National Park/Bar Harbor, ME **Ⓓ**

Hulls Cove Visitor Center
(207) 288–3338
Located at the park entrance, off ME 3 in Hulls Cove
☐ Acadia National Park/Bar Harbor, ME ⑩
☐ Saint Croix Island Int'l Hist. Site/Bar Harbor, ME ⑩

Cadillac Mountain Information Station
(207) 288–1204
Located at the top of the mountain
☐ Acadia National Park/Cadillac Mtn. ME ⑪
☐ Acadia National Park/Bar Harbor, Maine* ⑩
   *This cancellation features a minor variation from the similar
   Acadia/Bar Harbor cancellation: Maine instead of ME.*

Sieur de Monts Nature Center
(207) 288–3003
☐ Acadia National Park/Bar Harbor, ME ⑩

Thunder Hole Information Center
Located just past the Thunder Hole entrance station
☐ Acadia National Park/Thunder Hole, ME ⑪
☐ Acadia National Park/Bar Harbor, Maine ⑩

Blackwoods Ranger Station
(207) 288–3274
☐ Acadia National Park/Blackwoods Campground ⑪

Jordan Pond House Gift Shop
(207) 276–3244
☐ Acadia National Park/Jordan Pond, ME ⑪

Park Headquarters/Winter Visitor Center
(207) 288–3338
Located on Maine 233; join ME 233 at the park road junction at
the Cadillac Mountain entrance.
☐ Acadia National Park/Bar Harbor, ME ⑩
☐ Saint Croix Island Intl. Hist. Site/Red Beach, ME ⑪

Islesford Historical Museum

Little Cranberry Island
(207) 244–9224
The island is accessible by ferry and mail boat only; take the ferry from either the Northeast or the Southwest Harbors on Mount Desert Island.

☐ Acadia National Park/Islesford, ME Ⓤ

Seawall Campground Ranger Station

(207) 244–3600
From the Hull's Cove entrance, take ME 3 north to Maine 102, go south on ME 102 to its junction with Maine 102A, then take ME 102A to Seawall.

☐ Acadia National Park/Seawall Campground, ME Ⓤ

☐ Acadia National Park/Bar Harbor, ME Ⓓ

Schoodic Education and Research Center, Old Navy Station, Schoodic Peninsula

(207) 288–1318
The station is 60 miles from Bar Harbor. From the Hull's Cove entrance, take ME 3 north to U.S. Highway 1, and turn right/east. Follow US 1 to Maine 186. Turn right/south on ME 186, and follow the loop road to the end of the Schoodic Peninsula.

☐ Acadia National Park/Schoodic Peninsula, ME Ⓤ

☐ Acadia National Park/Bar Harbor, ME Ⓓ

Isle Au Haut Ranger Station

(207) 335–5551
Ferry details are provided in the Stamping tips section.

☐ Acadia National Park/Isle au Haut, ME Ⓤ

4 Saint Croix Island International Historic Site

Calais, Maine
(207) 288–3338
www.nps.gov/sacr

Number of cancellations: Three cancellations for Saint Croix Island, plus two cancellations for Acadia National Park at these locations

Difficulty: Tricky

About this site: The only International Historic Site in the National Park Service system, Saint Croix Island represents one of several European settlements in the United States that predate Jamestown—and, in this case, one that launched Canada's European history as well. Established in 1604 by Pierre Dugua, Sieur de Mons, Samuel Champlain, and seventy-seven others, Saint Croix was France's first attempt at year-round colonization on the frigid, generally inhospitable North Atlantic coast. Perhaps not surprisingly, the French moved on less than a year later, choosing a Nova Scotia inlet for long-term settlement in the New World. However, Saint Croix Island served as a home base and jumping-off point for Champlain, who went on to explore and chart the Bay of Fundy and the Atlantic coastline as far south as Cape Cod, Massachusetts.

Stamping tips: There are no cancellations at the park site itself—two of the Saint Croix Island cancellations are actually located at Acadia National Park visitor centers, while one resides in the town of Calais. The Calais cancellation is only available in the summer and early fall at the Downeast Heritage Museum, and the cancellation at Hulls Cove can be obtained only from the end of April through the end of October, so your stamping trip will need to be in summer or early fall to maximize your collection.

Don't miss this! As there is precious little to see here beyond a scenic view from the mainland of the island itself, and an interpretive trail lined with bronze statues of French settlers and Passamaquoddy ("People of the Dawn")—the native tribe that was the first to encounter the Frenchmen—some Passport enthusiasts might be tempted to skip an actual visit to this park.

The one-of-a-kind experience of this site, however, is in its sister site in Canada, just across the Saint Croix River in Bayside, New Brunswick. No other official National Park Service site has shared stewardship with another country, so you should take advantage of the opportunity to appreciate this unusual partnership firsthand. You'll find that the Canadian side of the park is not strikingly different from the American side (another outdoor interpretive trail), but the experience of being in another country, however briefly, is worth the effort. Bring your U.S. passport, your Social Security card, or a voter registration card as proof of citizenship—in our post-September 11 world, we're now required to prove ourselves as American citizens when we cross the Canadian border. While some border guards don't request this identification, it's wiser to carry it than to find yourself waylaid in a foreign country, even a friendly one, for hours or even days.

Hours: St. Croix Island International Historic Site is open dawn to dusk daily year-round on the American side. In winter, the statues along the interpretive trail are covered to protect them from the harsh weather.

The **Canadian side** is open June 1 to October 15, and can be visited at any time of day or night, as there is no staff assigned.

Hulls Cove Visitor Center is open April 15 through June, and in October, from 8:00 A.M. to 4:30 P.M. daily. In July and August, hours are 8:00 A.M. to 6:00 P.M. daily; in September, 8:00 A.M. to 4:30 P.M. daily. The visitor center is closed from November 1 to April 15.

Winter Visitor Center/Park Headquarters is open from November 1 to mid-April from 8:00 A.M. to 4:30 P.M. daily. It is closed Thanksgiving Day, Christmas Eve, Christmas Day, and New Year's Day. From mid-April to October 31, the center is open Monday to Friday, 8:00 A.M. to 4:30 P.M.

The **Downeast Heritage Museum** is open Memorial Day weekend through Columbus Day weekend from 10:00 A.M. to 5:00 P.M. daily. The museum is closed from mid-October through the end of May.

Fees: Admission is free at both the American and Canadian parks. Acadia charges $20.00 per car for a seven-day entrance permit; $5.00 per individual pedestrian, motorcyclist, or bicyclist for a seven-day entrance permit.

How to get there: The mainland unit at Red Beach is located on U.S. Highway 1, 8 miles south of Calais. There is no bridge to the island, nor are there any commercial ferries or other public transportation. If you wish to visit the island, you must bring your own boat.

Stamping Locations and What the Cancellations Say

Maine State Visitor Information Center/Downeast Heritage Museum

39 Union Street, Calais
(207) 454–2211

☐ Saint Croix Island Intl. Hist. Site/Calais, ME **①**

Acadia National Park Winter Visitor Center/Park Headquarters

(207) 288–3338
Located on Maine 233, which intersects the Park Loop Road at the Cadillac Mountain entrance

☐ Saint Croix Island Intl. Hist. Site/Red Beach, ME **①**

☐ Acadia National Park/Bar Harbor, ME **Ⓓ**

Acadia National Park, Hulls Cove Visitor Center

(207) 288–3338
Located off Maine 3 in Hulls Cove

☐ Saint Croix Island Int'l Hist. Site/Bar Harbor, ME **①**

☐ Acadia National Park/Bar Harbor, ME **Ⓓ**

Massachusetts

see map on pages 38–39

5 Adams National Historical Park

Quincy, Massachusetts
(617) 770–1175
www.nps.gov/adam

Number of cancellations: Two

Difficulty: Tricky

About this site: The nation's second and sixth presidents, John Adams and John Quincy Adams, were born not 75 yards from one another in Quincy, and they lived at the Old House at "Peace Field," the stately Colonial structure that served as the summer White House for both Adams presidents, and then as home to generations of their descendants.

Perhaps best known for his leadership in bringing the vote for American independence before the Second Continental Congress, John Adams was the first president to live in the White House, establishing residency there before the building was actually completed in 1800. His son, John Quincy Adams, served as a senator and the minister (ambassador) to Russia, becoming secretary of state under President James Monroe and working closely with him to form the Monroe Doctrine. As president, he created the first network of highways and canals that linked all sections of the United States.

Stamping tips: Adams National Historic Park closes from mid-November to mid-April; the house is not open for tours during this time, although the visitor center in Quincy keeps limited hours throughout the winter. A call before visiting is strongly encouraged.

While the visitor center provides the cancellation and inter-

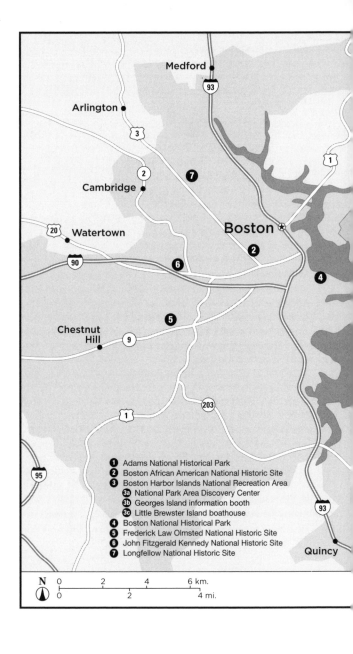

1 Adams National Historical Park
2 Boston African American National Historic Site
3 Boston Harbor Islands National Recreation Area
  3a National Park Area Discovery Center
  3b Georges Island information booth
  3c Little Brewster Island boathouse
4 Boston National Historical Park
5 Frederick Law Olmsted National Historic Site
6 John Fitzgerald Kennedy National Historic Site
7 Longfellow National Historic Site

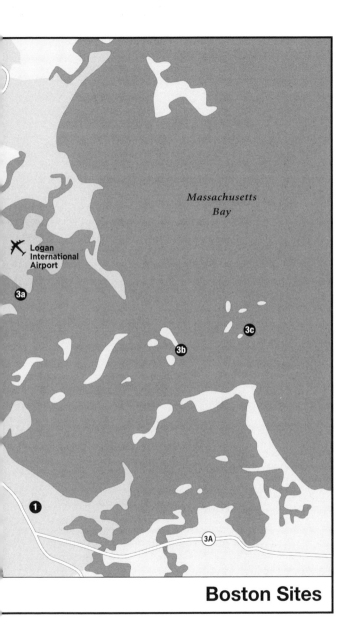

Massachusetts
Bay

Logan
International
Airport

3a

3c

3b

1

(3A)

Boston Sites

esting displays about the multigenerational Adams's accomplishments, the house and grounds make this trip worthwhile. If you come during the spring, summer, and fall, leave your backpack and other large carry-alls in the car—they're not permitted in the Adams house.

From the visitor center in Quincy, take the trolley that runs every thirty minutes on the quarter-hour to the "Old House," the home Adams named Peace Field. The trolley also runs to the birthplace of John and John Quincy Adams, which is within walking distance of the Quincy visitor center on Hancock Street.

Don't miss this! If you have a passion for Greek revival architecture as well as history, stop at the United First Parish Church, a working Unitarian church designed by renowned nineteenth-century architect Alexander Parris. This is the legendary "Old Stone Temple," now known colloquially as the Church of the Presidents, because both John and John Quincy Adams are entombed here, along with their wives, Abigail and Louisa Catherine Adams. The church's rich colonial history extends to John Hancock, the first signer of the Declaration of Independence, who was baptized here by his own father, one of the church's most distinguished reverends. A Unitarian parish since 1750, this church's congregation continues to honor the practice of liberal religion to this day. The church stands at 1306 Hancock Street, across from City Hall and a pleasant walk from the downtown visitor center.

Hours: From mid-April to mid-November, the Adams National Historic Park Visitor Center and Peace Field Contact Station are open daily from 9:00 A.M. to 5:00 P.M.

United First Parish Church is open Monday to Saturday from 9:00 A.M. to 5:00 P.M., and on Sunday from 1:00 to 5:00 P.M.

From mid-November to mid-April, the Adams National Historic Park Visitor Center is open Tuesday to Friday from 10:00 A.M. to 4:00 P.M.

Fees: $7.00 per adult for a seven-day admission pass. Children under sixteen are admitted free.

How to get there: From Boston traveling Interstate 93 or Massachusetts 128 south, take exit 7. Follow Massachusetts 3 south to Braintree and Cape Cod. Take the first exit off MA 3 south (exit 18 for Washington Street and the Quincy Adams "T"). Continue straight on Burgin Parkway through six traffic lights. At the seventh light, turn right onto Dimmock Street, and go one block to Hancock Street. Turn right onto Hancock Street. The visitor center, in the Galleria at President's Place, is at 1250 Hancock Street.

Stamping Locations and What the Cancellations Say

President's Place Galleria Visitor Center
1250 Hancock Street, Quincy
(617) 770–1175
☐ Adams Nat'l Historical Park/Quincy, MA ⓘ

Peace Field Contact Station at the 1873 Carriage House (the "Old House")
135 Adams Street, Quincy
(617) 745–0926
☐ Adams NHP Old House/Quincy, MA ⓘ

6 Boston African American National Historic Site

see map on pages 38–39
Boston, Massachusetts
(617) 742–5415
www.nps.gov/boaf

Number of cancellations: Two, plus one for the Underground Railroad

Difficulty: Easy

About this site: One of the largest communities of free African Americans lived in the vicinity of Beacon Hill, long before slavery was abolished. By 1800, some 1,100 New England Africans, freed slaves from the South and immigrants from the West Indies, called Boston home, working in jobs classified as unskilled or semiskilled: domestics, cooks, seamen, laborers, gardeners, waiters, and others. Most took these positions because they were the only jobs available to African Americans, even in New England. The most dangerous and dirtiest jobs on Boston's wharves were reserved for African-American workers, while in town, African-American men could find cleaner, less stressful work as porters. Some individuals rose above this stratification, however, and became successful entrepreneurs, attorneys, and authors. The 1.6-mile Black Heritage Trail® provides an inside look at the homes, churches, and meeting places that brought cohesion and a sense of community to this microcosm of Boston life.

❶ **Don't miss this!** The more I travel across the country, the more I realize how little I know about any culture's experience in living and working in America beyond my own Caucasian Jewish heritage. The insights I found at Boston African American National Historic Site dismissed many of my assumptions about African-American life in nineteenth-century New England—in essence, these free Americans were bound by class strictures that inhibited their education, their right to worship, and their ability to earn a comfortable living. So much for the "enlightened North" we read about in grammar school!

A walk down the Black Heritage Trail® showcases modest homes, the oldest African-American church in the United States, and a spectacular bronze sculpture by Augustus Saint-Gaudens honoring Robert Gould Shaw and the Massachusetts Fifty-fourth Regiment, the first all-African-American regiment to fight in the Civil War. Shaw died at twenty-five years old in a Civil War battle that took 270 of his men, while young William Carney, an African-American soldier from New Bedford, Massachusetts, ignored his own wounds and risked his life to save the Union flag. Carney became the first African-American man to receive the Congressional Medal of Honor.

Tales of bravery and the battle for liberty are everywhere on this trail, as the neighborhood's residents fought in times of war and at home during peacetime for rights every American deserves. Particularly striking are the George Middleton House, home of an unsung Revolutionary War hero; the Phillips School, a white high school that became a crucible of civil rights activism when African-American children were denied admission and shunted off to the overcrowded, underfunded Abiel Smith School down the street; the John J. Smith House, a haven for fugitive slaves before the Civil War began; and the Charles Street Meeting House, one of the first churches to attempt to integrate the races through religious observation.

Visitors can take the self-guided tour at any day or time, using the map and guide available at the visitor center and museum. Only the African Meeting House and the Abiel Smith School are open to the public.

Hours: The African Meeting House and Abiel Smith House are open year-round, Monday through Saturday, from 10:00 A.M. to 4:00 P.M. Guided tours of the Black Heritage Trail® are available Memorial Day through Labor Day during open hours.

Fees: Admission to this park is free.

How to get there: From the Massachusetts Turnpike (Interstate 90), take the Copley Square exit to Stuart Street, then turn left on Massachusetts 28 (Charles Street) to Boston Common.

To reach the site by MBTA subway, disembark at the Park Street stop on the Red and Green subway lines, or the Bowdoin Square stop on the Blue subway line.

Stamping Locations and What the Cancellations Say

Boston African American National Historic Site Visitor Center
15 Beacon Street
(617) 742–5415
☐ Boston African American National Historic Site/Boston, MA 🄳
☐ Boston Af Amer NHS/Underground RR Freedom Network 🄴

African Meeting House
46 Joy Street
(no phone)
☐ Boston African American National Historic Site/Boston, MA 🄳

7 Boston Harbor Islands National Recreation Area

see map on pages 38–39
Boston, Massachusetts
(617) 223–8666
www.nps.gov/boha

Number of cancellations: Four

Difficulty: Easy (or Heroic if you go for all three of the identical cancellations)

About this site: A relatively new addition to the national park system, established in 1996, Boston Harbor Islands form a land-and-water transitional corridor between the open sea and the mainland, with a knot of thirty-four islands reachable by ferry, tour boat, private craft, or sea kayak (for the experienced kayaker).

Recreational opportunities abound here, from hiking the well-worn trails to climbing Boston Light, a National Historic Landmark and one of the East Coast's oldest lighthouses. Swimming, boating, birding, boat trips to tour the harbor, and wildlife watching are all recommended activities here, while the islands also offer American and pre-American history to learn and explore. Twenty-one of the islands are designated part of an archeological district on the National Register of Historic Places because of the rich, 8,000-year-old Native American cultural heritage found beneath the surface. A 4,100-year-old human skeleton found in the 1960s has been confirmed as the oldest of its kind ever found in New England.

Stamping tips: The cancellations you will find at the Boston National Historic Park downtown visitor center are fluid and change with the seasons. If you're making a special trip to the visitor center just to get the Boston Harbor Islands uppercase cancellation, call first and ask the ranger it is under the desk—I got it there in late fall, but others have not obtained it during the spring, summer, and early fall.

You have a choice at this park: Take the easy route and collect one of the three identical cancellations on the mainland at Fan Pier, or be a hero and take two boat trips out to two different islands to acquire the two identical cancellations. Collecting the duplicate cancellations will require two separate trips, as tour boats do not travel between Georges and Little Brewster Islands. Reservations are recommended for all boat trips—and make careful note of the operating hours of the offices and landmarks you need to visit to get the cancellations.

Don't miss this! If you're not chasing imprints from every existing cancellation and you'd like to experience this park, you might choose a trip out to one or more of the ten visitor-friendly islands. The tiny, thirty-acre Bumpkin Island offers walking tours on flower-bordered paths, as well as rugged beaches full of shells. Parkland on Deer Island surrounds a wastewater treatment plant—perhaps not the most appealing backdrop for a picnic, but an excellent place for birding and other wildlife watching. Grape

Island's berry-laden fields attract abundant wildlife, and a climb to the top of Great Brewster Island's 100-foot dome reveals a view of four lighthouses along the coast.

If comprehensive cancellation stamp collecting is your goal, tour the Civil War–era Fort Warren on Georges Island, a military stronghold that served as both a training ground for Union troops and a prison for Confederate soldiers during the war. Recognized for humane treatment of its prisoners, Fort Warren nevertheless is haunted, they say, by the ghost of a prisoner's wife—a woman who aided an escape plot and was hanged in black robes for her crime. Georges Island provides a picnic ground, walking paths, and a snack bar, the only food service on the islands.

There's an additional reward if you make the trip out to Little Brewster Island—Boston Light, the first lighthouse in the United States, which participates in the United States Lighthouse Society stamp program. Get this bonus cancellation (it reads BOSTON LIGHT, with a lighthouse replacing the "I"), and tour the 1783 lighthouse, which operates to this day as an aid to navigation.

Hours: The park is open from 9:00 A.M. to sunset during the summer season. The islands are open on abbreviated schedules during the spring and fall; call the park for specific information about each island. The park is closed in winter.

Fees: There is no entrance fee, but there is a cost for transportation. Round-trip passenger fare is $10.00 for adults, $7.00 for seniors and children four to twelve, and free for children three and younger. The fare includes the ferry ride to Georges Island and water shuttles to five other islands.

How to get there: The islands are not accessible by car; you'll need to take a park ferry to reach them. Passenger ferries to Georges Island depart Boston at Long Wharf; from Hull at Pemberton Point; and from Quincy at Fore River Shipyard. A pdf file of the ferry schedules is available at www.bostonislands.org/trip_getthere.html. Tour boats and park shuttles leave from Georges Island for all but two other islands in the park; only Little Brewster and Thompson Islands are not accessible from Georges.

Boats to Little Brewster Island, home of Boston Light and one of the park's Passport cancellations, run from mid-June through early October and depart from the Fallon State Pier at Columbia Point. Departures times are Thursday at 10:00 A.M., and Friday at 10:00 A.M. and 2:00 P.M. Boats also run from Fan Pier at the South Boston Seaport on Saturday and Sunday at 10:00 A.M. and 2:00 P.M. Seating is limited to thirty-two people on these boats, so call (617) 223–8666 for reservations.

Stamping Locations and What the Cancellations Say

Boston National Historic Park downtown visitor center
15 State Street
(617) 242–5642
☐ BOSTON HARBOR ISLANDS/BOSTON, MA ❶
Cancellation located here in winter only

National Park Area Discovery Center
Fan Pier, Long Wharf
(617) 223–8666
☐ Boston Harbor Islands/Boston, MA ❷

Georges Island information booth
(617) 223–8666
☐ Boston Harbor Islands/Boston, MA ❷
Cancellation located here in summer only

Little Brewster Island boathouse
(617) 223–8666
☐ Boston Harbor Islands/Boston, MA ❶

8 Boston National Historic Park

See map on pages 38–39
Boston, Massachusetts
(617) 242–5642
www.nps.gov/bost

Number of cancellations: Six, including two slightly different Dorchester Heights cancellations

Difficulty: Tricky

About this site: I defy you to walk the Freedom Trail, down the still-cobbled streets and past the rows of buildings with names that awaken memories of history you learned before you could read, without murmuring the words of Longfellow's epic poem, *Paul Revere's Ride*: "On the eighteenth of April in seventy-five ..."

Nowhere are America's earliest days more richly preserved, and nowhere else on the eastern seaboard do the buildings ring so clearly with the clatter of colonial boots and the cries of rebellious patriots. From the Old North Church, where Paul Revere watched for the famous lights that signaled the start of the Revolutionary War, to the Old South Meeting House where Sam Adams rallied the locals to storm British ships at the Boston Tea Party, this citywide park is brimming with spirited tributes to the citizens whose tenacity gave this nation its start.

Stamping tips: Nearly all of the cancellations at this park are easily accessible, and the rangers are happy to direct visitors to them—and unusually congenial about digging through drawers and offices to find long retired or bonus cancellations for inquisitive Passport enthusiasts. Getting all of the cancellations in one day while enjoying this entire historic park requires some brisk walking—get an early start if you plan to take in most or all of the sixteen historic buildings, ships, and other sites along the trail. Allow at least a full afternoon to enjoy this park fully and collect all of the cancellations.

The main cancellation for Boston Harbor Islands usually arrives at the downtown visitor center for the winter around November, and remains until early April, when it returns to Long Wharf. Seasonal staff members are not always aware that this cancellation is available, so remember to ask for it.

The Faneuil Market cancellation is at the ranger's desk at the second-floor meeting hall.

Be sure to call ahead to schedule a tour of Dorchester Heights if you want to collect the cancellation there. Call (617) 242–5642 for reservations.

Don't miss this! Boston National Historic Park is nirvana for Revolutionary War buffs and other colonial period enthusiasts, but virtually any visitor will marvel at the accomplishments of the men and women who lived and defended their independence on these famous streets.

Start at Bunker Hill Monument, the site of the first major Revolutionary War battle. Exhibits at the base detail the events of June 17, 1775, when 1,500 colonial rebels slaughtered hundreds of British troops who marched head-on into battle. The American forces held their ground, despite the loss of more than half of their numbers, until their gunpowder ran out and they were forced to retreat—but not before they tore the British lines to shreds. Think carefully before you take the 294 steps to the top of the monument—the view of Boston below will satisfy, but you have a long walk down the Freedom Trail ahead (and don't believe anyone who tells you there's a cancellation at the top of the stairs—there isn't; case closed).

The USS *Constitution* (the famed "Old Ironsides") deserves attention, no matter how many tall ships you've toured in your travels. Still the oldest commissioned warship afloat in the world—in fact, it's listed in the *Guinness Book of World Records*—this remarkable ship saw battle in the War of 1812 and served as a training vessel throughout the Civil War. The tour includes opportunities to "go below," down slim ladders to the crew quarters, as well as a detailed explanation of her rigging, gun decks, food, and water storage that will satisfy any landlubber's curiosity.

If your time is limited, be sure to stop at the Old North Church and see the steeple in which sexton Robert Newman hung the "two if by sea" lights that told Paul Revere the British regulars approached by water on April 18, 1775, signaling the start of the Revolution. The Paul Revere House, the oldest house in downtown Boston, provides a suitably Spartan example of the colonial lifestyle, contrasting sharply with the American way of life Revere helped to make possible.

You'll need to stop for lunch, so make the most of the dozens of food vendors who crowd the stalls at Quincy Market. Stop upstairs at Faneuil Hall for the Passport cancellation and the ranger-led talk (given every half-hour, and well worth the time), and then head downstairs at Quincy Market for a lively meal of any nationality's cuisine, from Japanese to Jamaican—along with Boston's famous seafood, and plenty of it.

Finally, a stop at the Granary Burying Ground reveals the gravesites of Paul Revere, John Hancock, Samuel Adams, and the five men who perished in the Boston Massacre in 1770. The aging gravestones, with their hand-etched epitaphs, provide their own picture of life's fragility in this era of sudden gunfire, deadly battles, and hard-won triumphs.

Hours: Bunker Hill Lodge is open daily from 9:00 A.M. to 5:00 P.M. It is closed Thanksgiving, Christmas, and New Year's Day.

Charlestown Navy Yard Visitor Center is open daily from 9:00 A.M. to 5:00 P.M.

The downtown visitor center is open daily from 9:00 A.M. to 5:00 P.M.

The **Dorchester Heights Monument** is open for special ranger-guided tours. Call (617) 242–5642 for information.

The **USS *Constitution*** is open from April 1 to October 31, Tuesday through Sunday, 10:00 A.M. to 3:50 P.M. It is closed Monday. From November 1 to March 31, the ship is open Thursday through Sunday from 10:00 A.M. to 3:50 P.M., and is closed Monday, Tuesday, and Wednesday.

Faneuil Hall is open daily from 9:00 A.M. to 5:00 P.M., except when the City of Boston uses it for special events. It is closed Thanksgiving, Christmas, and New Year's Day.

Fees: Admission is free at all federally owned sites, including the Freedom Trail, Bunker Hill Monument, Dorchester Heights Monument, and USS *Constitution.* Ranger-led programs at the Freedom Trail and Faneuil Hall are also free.

Fees are collected at the privately owned and operated sites, including Old South Meeting House, Old State House, and Paul Revere House. These sites do not receive federal funding, and therefore do not accept the Federal Recreational Lands Pass for admission.

Old South Meeting House fees are $5.00 for adults, $4.00 for students and seniors, $1.00 for children six to eighteen, and free for children under six.

Old State House fees are $5.00 for adults, $4.00 for students and seniors, $1.00 for children six to eighteen, and free for children under six.

Paul Revere House fees are $3.00 for adults, $2.50 for seniors and college students, $1.00 for children five to seventeen, and free for children under five.

Discounted admissions for these three sites are $11.00 for adults, $3.00 for children six to eighteen.

How to get there: Public transportation is strongly recommended. The Massachusetts Bay Transportation Authority (MBTA) subway offers a fast, convenient alternative to driving—and an economical choice, as parking in Boston's ramp garages can run upwards of $23.00 per day. The Boston National Historic Park downtown visitor center, located at 15 State Street, is at the State Street stop of the Blue and Orange subway lines.

Water transportation runs frequently between downtown Boston (Long Wharf) and the Charlestown Navy Yard. For more information about Boston's excellent public transportation system, visit www.mbta.com.

If you must take your car, here's an alternative route to battling downtown traffic: Begin your visit at the Charlestown Navy Yards at the northern end of the Freedom Trail, where discounted parking with Boston National Historical Park validation is available from Nautica Parking Garage, located across from the park's visitor center on Constitution Road. To reach the navy yard from the south, take Interstate 93 north to exit 28/Sullivan Square. At the end of the ramp, turn right onto Cambridge Street, and proceed to the first light. Enter the traffic circle, and take the first right onto Rutherford Avenue. Move left, and at City Square, just before the bridge, turn left onto Chelsea Street.

From the north, take I–93 south to exit 28/Sullivan Square. Stay left on the exit ramp for about 0.3 mile. Proceed up the ramp to Rutherford Avenue. Follow the signs for RUTHERFORD AVE/ CITY SQUARE. Beyond Bunker Hill Community College, get into the left lane. Just before the bridge at City Square, turn left onto Chelsea Street.

Whether coming from the north or the south, once on Chelsea Street, follow these directions: At the first light, turn right onto Warren Street. Make the first left onto Constitution Road. The visitor center is at 55 Constitution Road on the right.

To reach Dorchester Heights from downtown Boston, travel south on I–93 (Southeast Expressway). Take the Mass Pike exit. Once on the exit ramp, bear left at the LOCAL sign. Take a left at the first set of lights onto Broadway. Follow Broadway to the fourth set of lights. Bear left onto East Broadway. Take the first right onto G Street, and the second right to Thomas Park. Dorchester Heights is on the left beyond South Boston High School.

Stamping Locations and What the Cancellations Say

Cancellations are listed as they would be found starting at the Bunker Hill Monument and Charlestown Navy Yard. If you begin at the downtown visitor center at 15 State Street, reverse the order of the locations.

Bunker Hill Lodge

(617) 242–5641

Located at the base of the Bunker Hill Monument, in Monument Square between Bartlett Street and High Street

☐ Boston National Historical Park/Bunker Hill Monument **Ⓤ**

Charlestown Navy Yard Visitor Center

55 Constitution Road

(617) 242–5601

☐ Boston National Historical Park/Charlestown Navy Yard **Ⓤ**

Faneuil Hall

3 Faneuil Hall Marketplace

(617) 242–5675

☐ Boston National Historical Park/Faneuil Hall **Ⓤ**

Downtown visitor center

15 State Street

(617) 242–5642

☐ Boston National Historical Park/Freedom Trail **Ⓤ**

☐ Dorchester Heights Nat. Hist. Site/Boston, MA **Ⓤ**

☐ BOSTON HARBOR ISLANDS/BOSTON, MA **Ⓓ**
   Available here from mid-November to early April only

Dorchester Heights Ranger Station

(617) 242–5642

☐ Dorchester Heights Nat'l Hist Site/Boston, MA **Ⓤ**

9 Cape Cod National Seashore

Wellfleet, Massachusetts
(508) 255–3421
www.nps.gov/caco

Number of cancellations: Three

Difficulty: Tricky

About this site: More than 43,000 acres of Atlantic Ocean shoreline—that's 40 linear, unbroken miles—form the coast of Cape Cod from Chatham to Provincetown, with beaches, salt marshes, upland, and forests extending along the Lower and Outer Cape. In summer, the hundreds of thousands of tourists who crowd the beaches can't hope to cover this pristine expanse; in the off-season, solitude seekers find satisfaction in long walks on the hard-packed sand.

Beyond the beach, salt marshes form a barrier between the ocean's force and human habitation, giving way to sparkling freshwater ponds as the park stretches inland. Hiking and biking trails—including the challenging Province Lands cycling trail, famous for its spectacular views across the drifting sand—provide travelers with adventure as well as solace. Lighthouses, pre-colonial history, even the first landfall of the passengers on the *Mayflower* all make Cape Cod National Seashore a legendary place, and one of the national park system's most popular ocean properties.

Stamping tips: With three cancellations at three visitor centers in different parts of the park, this should be easy to ace in one afternoon—and it is, if you travel during spring, summer, or early fall. The Province Lands Visitor Center closes for the winter. This is just another reminder that if you're traveling during the "fringe" times, between seasons, call your target stops beforehand to avoid disappointment. Note that the park headquarters in South Wellfleet is only open on weekdays, so be sure to stop on Friday if you're arriving for the weekend.

❶ **Don't miss this!** Bring your swimsuit, towel, sunscreen, and all of your beach paraphernalia. Start at Nauset Beach in Eastham and walk away from the crowds until you can't see any other people when you spread your towel out on the sand. Cape Cod's seashore is one of the few places in America where you can feel like you've slipped away to a deserted island, and you're all alone in paradise. Remember, however, that these mid-Atlantic waters are chilly-to-frigid, even on the warmest days, and often are subject to rip currents.

When you've had all the beach time you can handle, Cape Cod boasts three excellent biking trails, from easy to challenging. The Nauset Trail winds through wooded hills and past a marshy picnic area where northern bobwhites can be heard in spring, while the Head of the Meadow Trail offers a 2-mile ride in each direction, following the edge of a salt marsh from the beach to a freshwater lake. The Province Lands Trail is a 7-mile loop over rugged sand dunes, topping steep hills and dipping through low tunnels with surprise switchbacks in between—in summer, pedestrians are advised to watch out for speeding cyclists on this route. These seashore trails may be narrower than more recently constructed routes, so check at a visitor center for safety tips.

Whether or not you have ever owned a ham radio, the Marconi Station, 6 miles north of the Salt Pond Visitor Center, is a treat to visit. This is the exact spot where Guglielmo Marconi successfully completed the first U.S.-to-England wireless transmission in 1903, connecting President Theodore Roosevelt and King Edward VII of England. Marconi chose this site for its elevation as well as its emptiness of all other structures, and today it still offers a spectacular view of the ocean, despite overuse of the land when it served as an artillery training facility during World War II.

Hours: Parking lots throughout the park are open from 6:00 A.M. to midnight daily, year-round.

Salt Pond Visitor Center is open from 9:00 A.M. to 4:30 P.M. daily, year-round, with extended hours during the summer months.

Province Lands Visitor Center is open from 9:00 A.M. to 5:00 P.M. daily from early May through late October.

Park headquarters is open Monday through Friday from 8:00 A.M. to 4:30 P.M. It is closed on weekends and on all federal holidays.

Fees: Beach entrance fees are collected from late June through early September when lifeguards are on duty, and on weekends and holidays from Memorial Day to the end of September. The daily vehicle fee is $15.00, $3.00 for pedestrians and bicyclists. A pass good for a calendar year may be purchased for $45.00. Aside from the beaches, all facilities are free.

How to get there: From the Boston area, take Massachusetts 3 south to the Sagamore Bridge in Bourne. Follow U.S. Highway 6 eastward to Eastham and Provincetown.

From Providence, Rhode Island, take Interstate 95 north to Interstate 195. Follow US 6 eastward as described above.

Stamping Locations and What the Cancellations Say

Salt Pond Visitor Center
Off US 6 in Eastham
(508) 255–3421

☐ Salt Pond Visitor Center/Cape Cod National Seashore, MA **❶**

Cape Cod National Seashore Headquarters
South Wellfleet, off US 6 at the Marconi Station Site entrance
(508) 349–3785

☐ CAPE COD NATIONAL SEASHORE/MARCONI STATION
SITE, MA **❶**

Province Lands Visitor Center
Provincetown/Race Point
(508) 487–1256

☐ Cape Cod National Seashore/Provincelands Visitor
Center, MA **❶**

🔟 Essex National Heritage Area

Massachusetts NPS Affiliated Area
Salem, Massachusetts
(978) 740–0444
www.nps.gov/esse

Number of cancellations: Eleven cancellations for Essex, plus
two cancellations for Salem Maritime and one for Saugus Iron
Works

Difficulty: Challenging

About this site: Hundreds of years of history and culture come
together in this 40-mile stretch of the Massachusetts seaboard,
which begins 10 miles north of Boston and reaches to the Merrimack River on the southern New Hampshire border, and inland
all the way to Lowell. New England's rocky coasts and ocean
wildlife are only part of the total picture, as this area includes
some of the nation's earliest settlements, maritime centers, and
industrial sites, including both the Salem Maritime and Saugus
Iron Works National Historic Sites. Historic houses, museums,
and preserved lands feature prominently in this partnership of

federal, state, and local agencies, offering literally hundreds of activities for tourists in a 550-square-mile area.

Stamping tips: National Heritage Areas are organizations of affiliated sites and agencies that are run independently, and dissemination of National Heritage Area information can be spotty on the site level. Passport stamping in National Heritage Areas is a fairly new addition to the Passport program, so it's not uncommon to encounter information desk staff or volunteers who are entirely unfamiliar with your Passport, and who are dead certain that there is no cancellation available at their site. Be persistent in as polite a manner as you can manage—the cancellation is most likely there, but may be kept in its original box in a cabinet or hidden away in a desk drawer. Encourage the staff member to look around a bit, or to ask someone in an office-level position if an Essex National Heritage Area cancellation is available. Your persistence will help educate the front-line staff member and will raise awareness of the program. But be sure to keep your interaction as pleasant as possible, to increase the staff's enthusiasm for Passport-wielding tourists.

When you're planning your stamping run through this area, note that the Newburyport Chamber of Commerce is open Monday to Friday, and that several of the visitor centers are closed from late fall through early spring. Gloucester, Haverhill, and Ipswich all close for the winter, so a successful stamping excursion must be completed between the months of May and October—and most likely on a weekend, as several sites are closed on Monday, Tuesday, and/or Wednesday in the off-season.

Don't miss this! With so many sites and attractions in this heritage area, it's difficult to choose just one or two to highlight. Every family member will find something appealing here. Be sure to visit the in-depth site at www.essexheritage.org to plan your visit before traveling.

The Witch House and associated sites in Salem offer family fun and a shocking look at the trials that made the term "witch hunt"—an out-of-control, hysteria-based search for guilty parties to an imagined crime—part of the American lexicon. While much of Salem's witch district is ticky-tacky and cartoon-like at best, the dramatic retelling of the witch trial story truly moves audiences.

You can also satisfy your curiosity about seventeenth- and eighteenth-century history and architecture during your visit, from the Manchester Historic District with its three centuries of popular architectural styles to individually preserved homes in Newbury and Beverly. Virtually every community in the heritage area has made an effort to preserve a portion of its colonial history in small museums, many of them in converted historic buildings, so if you visit on a rainy or snowy day, there are plenty of chances to amble through rooms filled with artifacts from the 1600s and 1700s, and to chat with experts on the landmarks and events that shaped this region's development.

For outdoor fun, Essex National Heritage Area prides itself on its efforts to preserve open land for use by more than 400 species of birds and many small animals. Hike, bike, or go birding through one or more of the farms, beaches, and refuges protected here. In particular, Newburyport Harbor and its accompanying Parker River (Plum Island) National Wildlife Refuge offer some of the best birding for rare and unusual water-loving birds in the Northeast, with regular sightings of the endangered piping plover, as well as peregrine falcon, rough-legged hawk, and wintering loons, grebes, and sea ducks.

Hours: Hours vary by individual sites and attractions. Stamping site hours are listed below.

Gloucester Visitor Center is open July to September from 9:00 A.M. to 6:00 P.M. daily. In May, June, and October, the center is open 9:00 A.M. to 6:00 P.M. Thursday to Sunday, and closed Monday to Wednesday. It is closed November to mid-May.

Haverhill Visitor Center is open from Memorial Day to Halloween from 10:00 A.M. to 5:00 P.M., Tuesday to Sunday. It is closed Monday. It is closed in winter.

Ipswich Visitor Center is open from Memorial Day to Columbus Day from 9:00 A.M. to 5:00 P.M. from Monday through Saturday, and from noon to 5:00 P.M. on Sunday. It is closed in winter.

Lawrence Visitor Center is open daily year-round from 9:00 A.M. to 4:00 P.M. It is closed Thanksgiving, Christmas, and New Year's Day.

Lynn Visitor Center is open year-round Monday through Saturday from 1:00 to 4:00 P.M. It is closed Sunday.

Newburyport Chamber of Commerce Visitor Center is open year-round Monday through Friday from 9:00 A.M. to 5:00 P.M. It is closed Saturday and Sunday.

Peabody Visitor Center is open year-round Monday through Saturday from 10:00 A.M. to 3:00 P.M., and on Sunday from noon to 3:00 P.M.

Salem Visitor Center is open daily from 9:00 A.M. to 5:00 P.M. It is closed Thanksgiving, Christmas, and New Year's Day.

The **Maria Miles visitor center** is open daily from 8:00 A.M. to 8:00 P.M.; it remains open until 10:00 P.M. from Memorial Day through Columbus Day.

Saugus Iron Works National Historic Site Visitor Center is open from April 1 through October 31 daily from 9:00 A.M. to 5:00 P.M. It is open from November 1 to March 31 daily from 9:00 A.M. to 4:00 P.M. It is closed Thanksgiving, Christmas, and New Year's Day.

Fees: Fees vary at each individual site; call the desired site or attraction for information.

How to get there: Major highways are Interstates 93, 95, and 495, U.S. Highway 1, and Massachusetts 128. There are a number of scenic roads through the area and along the shore. Download a map from the Essex National Heritage Area Web site at www.essexheritage.org.

If you're exploring the entire Essex historic area and you'd like to visit all of the centers and collect all ten cancellations, here are directions to each:

Saugus Iron Works National Historic Site Visitor Center: From I–95, take exit 43 (Walnut Street). Drive east toward Lynn, and follow the brown National Park Service signs for 3.5 miles to the iron works. The center is at 244 Central Street.

Lynn Visitor Center/Lynn Heritage State Park: From the north, take MA 128/I–95 south to exit 44 for US 1 south. Take the first exit to Massachusetts 129 east. Follow MA 129 east to downtown Lynn. Beyond the MBTA commuter rail trestle, you will find the visitor center on the opposite left corner. The address is 590 Washington Street.

From the south and west, take MA 128/I–95 north to exit 44B. Follow MA 129 east to downtown Lynn; use directions above.

From Salem, take U.S. Highway 1A south to Lynn. At the North Shore Community College, take a sharp right onto Union Street, then a right onto Washington Street. Parking and the visitor center are on the left.

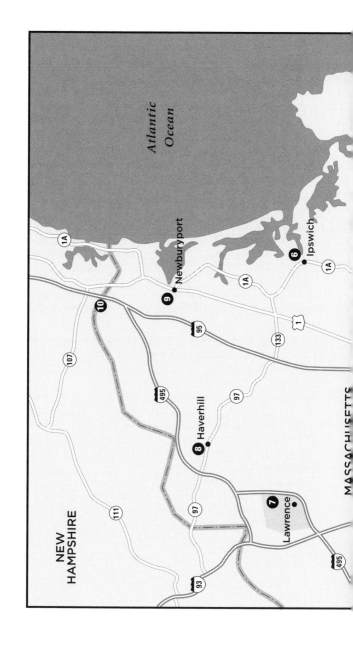

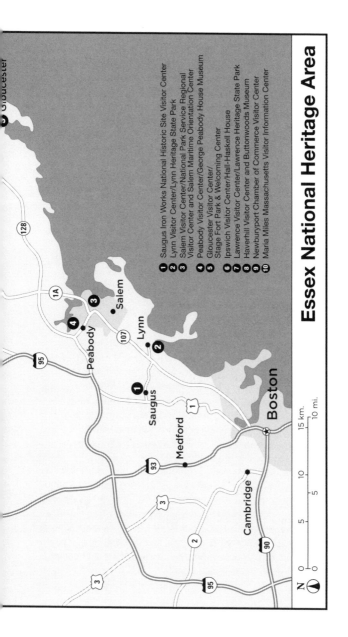

Essex National Heritage Area

1. Saugus Iron Works National Historic Site Visitor Center
2. Lynn Visitor Center/Lynn Heritage State Park
3. Salem Visitor Center/National Park Service Regional Visitor Center and Salem Maritime Orientation Center
4. Peabody Visitor Center/George Peabody House Museum
5. Gloucester Visitor Center/ Stage Fort Park & Welcoming Center
6. Ipswich Visitor Center/Hall-Haskell House
7. Lawrence Visitor Center/Lawrence Heritage State Park
8. Haverhill Visitor Center and Buttonwoods Museum
9. Newburyport Chamber of Commerce Visitor Center
10. Maria Miles Massachusetts Visitor Information Center

From Boston, take US 1A north to Lynnway. Turn left, following US 1A onto Market Street, then turn right onto Broad Street. At the North Shore Community College, bear left onto Union Street; take the next right onto Washington Street. Parking and the visitor center are on the left.

Salem Maritime Orientation Center: From MA 128, take exit 25A/Massachusetts 114 east to Salem. Follow MA 114 into Salem, where it will become North Street, then Summer Street (pass the Witch House on the right). Turn left onto Norman Street, and then stay straight onto Derby Street. The Salem Maritime Orientation Center is at 193 Derby Street.

Salem Visitor Center/National Park Service Regional Visitor Center: From Salem Maritime Orientation Center, follow Derby Street straight past Beverly Cooperative Bank (MA 114 will turn right at this corner toward Marblehead). At the next intersection, turn left onto Hawthorne Boulevard. At the light, turn left onto Essex Street. The visitor center is at the end of Essex Street on the right corner, at the corner of Essex and New Liberty. The address is 2 New Liberty Street. There is a pay-parking garage across the street from the visitor center.

Peabody Visitor Center/George Peabody House Museum: Follow MA 128 to exit 28 for Centennial Drive in Peabody. Turn left onto Centennial Drive, and then right onto Summit Street. Follow Summit to the light, and turn left onto Washington Street. Follow Washington for 2.5 miles to the George Peabody House Museum, which is on the left at 205 Washington Street.

Gloucester Visitor Center/Stage Fort Park & Welcoming Center: Driving north from Beverly and Manchester-by-the-Sea on Massachusetts 127, Stage Fort Park will be on the right. There are two entrances, so if you drive past the first one, you go around the bend to the second.

From MA 128, take exit 14 for Massachusetts 133 east to Gloucester. Follow MA 133 (and the brown ENHC signs) to its end, and turn right onto MA 127 south. Stage Fort Park is immediately on your left. The visitor center is on Hough Street.

Ipswich Visitor Center/Hall-Haskell House: From MA 128 north or south, take exit 20 for US 1A north, and follow it through North Beverly, Hamilton, and Wenham into Ipswich. The visitor center is on the right at 36 South Main Street (US 1A).

From I–95, take exit 54 for MA 133 east, and follow MA 133 to US 1A south. The visitor center is south of downtown on the left.

Lawrence Visitor Center/Lawrence Heritage State Park: From I–495, take exit 45 (Marston Street). Take the first left onto Canal Street. Go straight through lights, then take the second right onto Jackson Street. The visitor center will be on the right at 1 Jackson Street.

Haverhill Visitor Center and Buttonwoods Museum: From I–95, take exit 53 for Massachusetts 97 west (slightly more direct/faster) or exit 54 for MA 133 west. MA 133 hooks into MA 97 in downtown Georgetown. Follow MA 97 over the Merrimack River and into Haverhill. MA 97 turns left shortly after crossing the Merrimack, and then it's a straight shot to the visitor center, which is about 1.5 miles down on the right at 240 Water Street (MA 97/Massachusetts 113).

From I–495, take exit 51 for Massachusetts 125, and head south into Haverhill to the intersection with MA 97. Go east to the visitor center.

Newburyport Chamber of Commerce Visitor Center: From I–95, take exit 57 for MA 113 east. Follow MA 113 for 2.5 miles to Green Street. Turn left onto Green Street. Follow Green to its end; the parking lot is across the street diagonally. The office is at 38R Merrimac Street.

Maria Miles visitor center: The center is on I–95 southbound at exit 60 in Salisbury. Heading southbound on I–95, take exit 60 (just before the Massachusetts/New Hampshire border).

Going northbound on I–95, take exit 1 in New Hampshire, turn left on New Hampshire 107, go under the interstate, and take the first right to return to I–95, now going south. Then take exit 60.

Stamping Locations and What the Cancellations Say

The sites are listed in the order you would reach them if you drive north from Boston to the New Hampshire border. If you're coming south from New Hampshire, simply reverse the order.

Saugus Iron Works National Historic Site Visitor Center
244 Central Street, Saugus
(781) 233–0050
☐ Essex National Heritage Area/Saugus, MA ⓤ
☐ Saugus Iron Works NHS/Saugus, MA ⓤ

Lynn Visitor Center/Lynn Heritage State Park
590 Washington Street, Lynn
(781) 592–2465
☐ Essex National Heritage Area/Lynn, MA ⓤ

Salem Visitor Center/National Park Service
Regional Visitor Center
2 New Liberty Street, Salem
(978) 740–1650
☐ Essex National Heritage Area/Salem, MA ⓞ
☐ SALEM MARITIME NATIONAL HIST SITE/SALEM, MA ⓤ

Salem Maritime Orientation Center
193 Derby Street, Salem
(978) 740–1660
☐ Essex National Heritage Area/Salem, MA ⓞ
☐ Salem Maritime National Hist. Site/Salem MA ⓤ

Peabody Visitor Center/George Peabody House Museum
205 Washington Street, Peabody
(978) 531–0355
☐ Essex National Heritage Area/Peabody, MA ⓤ

Gloucester Visitor Center/Stage Fort Park & Welcoming Center
Hough Street, Gloucester
(978) 281–8865
☐ Essex National Heritage Area/Gloucester, MA ⓤ

Ipswich Visitor Center/Hall-Haskell House
36 South Main Street, Ipswich
(978) 356–8540
☐ Essex National Heritage Area/Ipswich, MA ⓤ

Lawrence Visitor Center/Lawrence Heritage State Park
1 Jackson Street, Lawrence
(978) 794–1655
☐ Essex National Heritage Area/Lawrence, MA ⓞ

Haverhill Visitor Center and Buttonwoods Museum
240 Water Street, Haverhill
(978) 374–4626
☐ Essex National Heritage Area/Haverhill, MA ⓞ

Newburyport Chamber of Commerce Visitor Center
38R Merrimac Street, Newburyport
(978) 462–6680
☐ Essex National Heritage Area/Newburyport, MA ⓞ

Maria Miles Massachusetts Visitor Information Center
(978) 465–6333 or (978) 465–6555
☐ Essex National Heritage Area/Salisbury, MA ⓞ

🟦11 Frederick Law Olmsted National Historic Site

see map on pages 38–39
Brookline, Massachusetts
(617) 566–1689
www.nps.gov/frla
Number of cancellations: One
Difficulty: Tricky
About this site: Considered the founder of American landscape architecture, Frederick Law Olmsted and his staff designed virtually all of the nation's most beloved parks, including Central Park and Prospect Park in New York City, the Boston and Buffalo, New York, park systems, and the grounds of the White House and the U.S. Capitol. His well-preserved home and office contains more than one million documents detailing the firm's work on approximately 5,000 landscapes throughout the country.

The estate, known as Fairsted, is undergoing major construction and will be closed to the public until fall 2010.

Stamping tips: When construction activity permits, collectors may go to the main entrance and ask for the cancellation. Management recommends that you call ahead or check the park Web site before making a trip to the site, but will make every effort to accommodate you.

Normally, the Olmstead site is open only from June through October. New hours will be posted on the Web site when the site reopens.

Don't miss this! If you've managed to get the cancellation despite the construction and you'd like to experience something representative of this park's significance, take a ranger-guided tour of some of the parks Olmsted designed in Boston. These parks, known as Boston's "emerald necklace," include the Back Bay Fens, Riverway, Olmsted Park, Jamaica Ponds, Arnold Arboretum, and Franklin Park—fine examples of Olmsted's ability to create naturalistic green spaces within major metropolitan areas. Call the site's phone number or visit the Web site for more information about these tours.

Hours: Currently closed; check the Web site at www.nps.gov/frla for reopening information. Normally, the park is open daily year-round, with tours offered Friday through Sunday between 10:00 A.M. and 4:30 P.M.

Fees: Admission is free for all visitors.

How to get there: From Boston and points east, follow Huntington Avenue southwest from the area of Copley Square. Continue on Huntington Avenue as it becomes Massachusetts 9/Boylston Street in Brookline. At the third major intersection, turn left onto Warren Street, and follow it one-eighth of a mile to the intersection of Warren and Dudley Streets. The historic site is on the right corner.

From Interstate 95/Massachusetts 128 and points west, take exit 20 (MA 9 east to Boston/Brookline). Follow MA 9/Boylston Street for approximately 5 miles. Pass through a major intersection with Lee Street, and continue on Boylston, passing the Brookline Reservoir. At the next intersection, turn right onto Warren Street, and follow directions from Warren Street given above.

Stamping Locations and What the Cancellations Say

Frederick Law Olmsted National Historic Site information desk

99 Warren Street, Brookline
Closed until fall 2010

☐ Frederick Law Olmsted Nat'l Hist Site/Brookline, MA ⓿

---

12 John Fitzgerald Kennedy National Historic Site

See map on pages 38–39
Brookline, Massachusetts
(617) 566–7937
www.nps.gov/jofi

Number of cancellations: One

Difficulty: Tricky

About this site: Our thirty-fifth president was born in these modest surroundings, the first home of Joseph and Rose Kennedy and the place where young John spent his childhood. Many mementos collected by the Kennedys are displayed here, and while some of the furnishings are not original to the house, the president's mother selected them when she redecorated the house in the 1960s as a memorial to her son. President Kennedy was assassinated in Dallas, Texas, on November 22, 1963.

Stamping tips: This historic site is only open during the spring and summer months. Call or check the Web site before visiting to be sure that the house is open.

❶ **Don't miss this!** When the Kennedy home became a national park site, Rose Fitzgerald Kennedy and her staff made considerable effort to return many of the original furnishings to the home. Visitors can see a little table for two in the dining room at which young Jack Kennedy often sat with his older brother, Joseph P. Kennedy, Jr. One of Rose and Joe's favorite wedding gifts, a piano, found its way back to the home as well.

Passport cancellation collector Coleen Tighe of Somerset County, New Jersey, told me that she was struck by the small index cards Rose Kennedy kept on her children's health history, including their height and weight at specific intervals and their vaccination records. The cards' content serves as a reminder of the advances in health care we have enjoyed since the 1930s, when Rose faced the same daily challenges every mother encounters as she protected her children from disease.

Hours: In season (early May through mid-September), the park is open Wednesday through Sunday from 10:00 A.M. to 4:30 P.M. Check the Web site for the current season's opening dates and hours. Tours of the museum space are given every half-hour during most of the season; in the fall, tour times are given hourly.

Fees: $3.00 for adults; this includes the ranger-guided house tour. Children eighteen and under are admitted free. Fees may increase in 2008.

How to get there: From Interstate 90/Massachusetts Turnpike, exit at Allston/Brighton/Cambridge. Take the Allston/Brighton off-ramp, merge onto Cambridge Street, and follow it 0.75 mile. At the second stoplight, turn left onto Harvard Street. Follow Harvard Street 0.75 mile across major intersections with Brighton Avenue and Commonwealth Avenue. Turn left onto Beals Street, and go three-quarters of a block to 83 Beals Street.

Stamping Locations and What the Cancellations Say

John F. Kennedy National Historic Site bookstore
Located in the basement of the house

☐ John F. Kennedy Nat'l Hist. Site/Brookline, MA ❶

⓭ John H. Chafee Blackstone River Valley National Heritage Corridor

Massachusetts NPS Affiliated Area
Woonsocket, Rhode Island (headquarters)
(401) 762–0250
www.nps.gov/blac

Number of cancellations: One in Massachusetts (four additional duplicates available in Rhode Island)

Difficulty: Tricky

About this site: Covering 400,000 acres and stretching from the Blackstone River in Worcester, Massachusetts, to Narragansett Bay in Providence, Rhode Island, this heritage corridor commemorates the influence of the Blackstone River's water power—

generated by a 438-foot drop over 46 miles—on the growth of industry in this region. The first water-powered cotton-spinning factory, built by Sam Slater, harnessed the power of the river and set off a rush of mill construction that turned this area into a booming industrial landscape.

Don't miss this! The park that surrounds this visitor center offers many recreational opportunities that combine a little history with a fine walk, canoe paddle, or bike ride along the river or the Blackstone Canal. You'll see the remains of a canal lock, dams, bridges, worker housing, and a company store from the days when this canal provided central Massachusetts with access to the Atlantic Ocean.

Hours: Blackstone River and Canal Heritage Park is open sunrise to sunset year-round. The visitor center is open from 10:00 A.M. to 4:00 P.M. daily.

Hours vary at other Blackstone River Valley sites. Visit www.nps.gov/blac/home.htm for information about specific parks, refuges, buildings, and other attractions throughout the corridor.

Fees: Fees vary by site for the more than 500 locations throughout the corridor. Visit www.nps.gov/blac/home.htm for detailed information.

How to get there: Massachusetts 146 is the main highway running north and south between Providence and Worcester, with major intersections with Interstates 95 and 295 in Rhode Island. Exit 11 on Interstate 90 (Massachusetts Turnpike) will give access to Massachusetts 122 and visitor information centers in Worcester and Uxbridge.

The stamping location at River Bend Farm Visitor Center is in Blackstone River and Canal Heritage State Park in Uxbridge, which is open daily. Uxbridge is in the south-central portion of the state, at the junction of Massachusetts 16 and MA 122. From the Massachusetts Turnpike, take exit 11, and follow MA 122 south to North Uxbridge. At the traffic lights, turn left onto East Hartford Avenue, then take a right turn onto Oak Street. The park is at 287 Oak Street.

From MA 146, take MA 16 east to Uxbridge Center, and turn left onto MA 122 north. In 1.5 miles, turn right at the traffic light onto East Hartford Avenue. In 1 mile, turn right at the Tri-River Family Health Center onto Oak Street.

Stamping Locations and What the Cancellations Say

River Bend Farm Visitor Center
287 Oak Street, Uxbridge
(508) 278–7604

☐ Blackstone River Valley Nat'l Heritage Corridor/
Massachusetts & Rhode Island ➊

14 Longfellow National Historic Site

see map on pages 38–39
Cambridge, Massachusetts
(617) 876–4491
www.nps.gov/long

Number of cancellations: One, plus one for the Underground
Railroad

Difficulty: Tricky

About this site: Henry Wadsworth Longfellow, perhaps the best-
loved American poet and a trailblazer whose work helped create
a uniquely American literary style, lived in this Georgian-style historic mansion from 1837 to 1882. The author of some of the most
familiar poetry in the American lexicon—*Paul Revere's Ride,
Song of Hiawatha, The Wreck of the Hesperus,* and *Evangeline*
among them—Longfellow opened his home to many contemporaries who were literary or artistic giants in their own right,
notably Ralph Waldo Emerson, Nathanial Hawthorne, Julia Ward
Howe, Charles Dickens, Henry James, Anthony Trollope, and
Oscar Wilde. Longfellow received this 1759 mansion as a wedding gift from his wife's father in 1843. General George Washington also used it as a headquarters and base of operations in
1775 and 1776.

Stamping tips: The house and visitor center close to walk-in traffic during the winter, and are only open Wednesday to Sunday
from May or June through October. The gardens and grounds are
open from dawn to dusk every day of the year.

➊ **Don't miss this!** Of the many original furnishings used by
Longfellow, many of the most interesting are in the poet's study.
You'll see the chair created from the wood of a "spreading chest-
nut tree" presented to Longfellow by Cambridge schoolchildren

on his seventy-second birthday, in appreciation of one of his most famous works, *The Village Blacksmith*.

Many of the tour guides at this park can recite Longfellow's poetry from memory—and it's a treat to hear this lyrical, narrative verse spoken aloud.

Hours: From May or June to October, hours are Wednesday to Sunday from 10:00 A.M. to 4:30 P.M. Check the Web site for opening dates. Guided tours (the only way to see the house) are at 10:30 and 11:00 A.M., and at 1:00, 2:00, 3:00, and 4:00 P.M.

Fees: $3.00 for adults sixteen and older; children fifteen and under are admitted free.

How to get there: From Interstate 90/Massachusetts Turnpike, take the Allston/Cambridge exit toward Cambridge. Cross the bridge, and turn left onto Memorial Drive. Follow Memorial Drive past the major intersection with John F. Kennedy Street, and bear right onto Hawthorne Street. Take the next left onto Mount Auburn Street and the next right onto Willard Street. Turn right onto Brattle Street at the next intersection. Longfellow National Historic Site is on your immediate left at 105 Brattle Street.

Parking at the site is not available, except for vehicles with handicapped parking permits. Limited metered parking is available on Brattle Street. Consider taking an MBTA Red Line train to Alewife Station; get off at Harvard Square and walk a short distance up Brattle Street to the site.

Stamping Locations and What the Cancellations Say

Longfellow National Historic Site Visitor Center
105 Brattle Street, Cambridge

☐ Longfellow National Historic Site/Cambridge, MA ❶
☐ Longfellow NHS/Underground RR Freedom Network ❶

🔢 Lowell National Historical Park

Lowell, Massachusetts
(978) 970–5000
www.nps.gov/lowe

Number of cancellations: Two
Difficulty: Easy

About this site: These meticulously preserved textile mills commemorate America's move to mechanization during the Industrial Revolution in the late 1800s. The operating weave room at the Boott Cotton Mills Museum contains eighty-eight working looms, and serves as a cogent illustration of the role of working women in the nineteenth century. Worker housing for the "mill girls," commercial buildings, and interpretive exhibits provide a look back into the history of labor and technology's introduction into the working world.

Don't miss this! Call me a feminist (please!), but the most fascinating things I found in Lowell were the stories of women's lives in this "cathedral of industry," a place where women earned their own livings and enjoyed their discretionary income. Their eagerness to send money home to help their families, their pride in their earning abilities, and their courage in creating one of the first labor unions makes these independent, industrious women fine role models for our twenty-first-century daughters.

Hours: Lowell National Historic Park is open year-round.

The visitor center is open from the end of November to early March, Monday to Saturday, from 9:00 A.M. to 4:30 P.M., and Sunday from 10:00 A.M. to 4:30 P.M. From March through the end of November, the center is open daily from 9:00 A.M. to 5:00 P.M. The center is closed Thanksgiving, Christmas, and New Year's Day.

Boott Cotton Mills Museum is open from Thanksgiving weekend to the beginning of March, Monday to Friday, from 10:00 A.M. to 2:00 P.M.; Saturday, holidays, and school vacation weeks from 9:30 A.M. to 4:30 P.M.; and Sunday from 11:00 A.M. to 4:30 P.M. From early March through the end of November, the museum is open daily from 9:30 A.M. to 4:30 P.M. The museum is closed Thanksgiving, Christmas Eve, Christmas Day, and New Year's Day.

Fees: Admission to Boott Cotton Mills Museum is $6.00 for adults, good for seven days; $4.00 for seniors and students with valid school identification; $3.00 for children six to sixteen; and free for children five and under.

There is no cost for the visitor center and the Mill Girls and Immigrants exhibit.

How to get there: Take the Lowell Connector from either Interstate 495 (exit 35C) or U.S. Highway 3 (exit 30A if traveling southbound, exit 30B if traveling northbound). Follow the connector to Thorndike Street (exit 5B). On Thorndike Street, which becomes Dutton Street, continue straight through four traffic lights. At the fifth traffic light, turn right off Dutton Street into the visitor parking lot. From the lot, walk through the mill archways and courtyard to the visitor center in the building on the far side of the courtyard.

Stamping Locations and What the Cancellations Say

Lowell National Historic Park visitor center
246 Market Street
(978) 970-5000

☐ Lowell Nat'l Historical Park/Lowell, MA ⓓ

Boott Cotton Mills Museum
115 John Street

☐ Lowell Nat'l Historical Park/Lowell, MA ⓓ

16 Minute Man National Historical Park

Concord, Massachusetts
(978) 369–6993
www.nps.gov/mima

Number of cancellations: Three, plus one for the Underground Railroad

Difficulty: Tricky

About this site: Paul Revere warned that the regulars were coming on the night before the American Revolution began, riding from Charlestown to Lincoln to alert the American "minutemen"—men chosen from the militia's ranks for their enthusiasm and reliability, and who always arrived first when the alarm was sounded. After the catalytic battle at the North Bridge, the colonial militia fired on the British for 16 miles, from Merian's Corner back to Boston Harbor. The colonists' ability to rout the redcoats set the stage for climactic battles throughout the Revolution.

Stamping tips: While the North Bridge Visitor Center is open all year (although hours are limited each day from the end of November through March 31), the Minute Man Visitor Center and The Wayside close for the winter. The best time to visit this park to get all the cancellations in one trip is from late May through the end of October.

Thanks to a bit of luck, Nic and I made a mid-November visit to the Minute Man Visitor Center on the very day and at the very time that a U.S. military band was scheduled to give a concert in the center's lobby. We slipped in, found the cancellation stamp and ink pad on the counter, and surreptitiously stamped our Passport before slipping back out to enjoy more of the park. These are the neat little moments that make Passport stamping so much fun, but they can hardly be considered reliable ways to obtain a cancellation. Make your visit between the Saturday before Memorial Day and the last weekend in October for the best results.

Don't miss this! Stand in the exact spot where a newly American soldier fired "the shot heard round the world." If you listen closely, you'll hear the echo of British regulars' boots as they marched into unforeseen resistance at the North Bridge. Imagine standing with that first United States regiment and defending your right to life, liberty, and the pursuit of happiness against a uniformed, well-trained, organized army of the king's finest men...and fighting with such spirit that the British had no choice but to die or retreat. Feel the passion of that moment, and know what coursed through the veins of hundreds of minutemen and militiamen when they drove off the redcoats and scored the first victory for America.

You man also visit The Wayside, the home of nineteenth-century American writer Nathaniel Hawthorne (author of *The House of the Seven Gables* and *The Scarlet Letter*) and the childhood home of Louisa May Alcott (who wrote *Little Women, Little Men,* and *Eight Cousins*). Finally preserved by the daughter of Margaret Sidney (the pen name of Harriett Lothrop, author of the *Five Little Peppers* series), this is the only home in the national park system that was owned by three literary families, and the uniquely American literary voice that developed here is considered Concord's "Second Revolution."

Hours: North Bridge Visitor Center is open daily from the end of November through March 31 from 11:00 A.M. to 3:00 P.M. From April 1 through the Sunday after Thanksgiving it is open from 9:00 A.M. to 5:00 P.M. It is closed Thanksgiving, Christmas, and New Year's Day.

Minute Man Visitor Center is open April 1 to the end of October from 9:00 A.M. to 5:00 P.M. and from 9:00 A.M. to 4:00 P.M. from the beginning of November to the Sunday after Thanksgiving. It is closed late November through March.

The Wayside is open from late May through October for tours only on Friday, Saturday, and Sunday at 11:00 A.M., 1:30 P.M., 3:00 P.M., and 4:30 P.M.

Fees: Admission is free at Minute Man National Historical Park. Admission to The Wayside is $5.00 for adults and free to children sixteen and under.

How to get there: From Interstate 95, take exit 30B onto Massachusetts 2A west. The Minute Man Visitor Center 0.5 mile west of the interstate ramp. From the Massachusetts Turnpike, take the I–95 exit (exit 14), and follow the directions above.

To reach The Wayside, continue west on Massachusetts Avenue (MA 2A) to Lexington Road. Turn right on Lexington; The Wayside is a large yellow house on the right with a parking area across the street. The address is 455 Lexington Road in Concord.

To reach the North Bridge Visitor Center, continue west on Lexington Road, and turn right on Monument Street. Take Monument to Liberty Street; turn left. The visitor center is at 174 Liberty Street.

Stamping Locations and What the Cancellations Say

Minute Man Visitor Center
(781) 674–1920
☐ Minute Man NHP/Concord & Lexington, MA ⓤ

North Bridge Visitor Center
174 Liberty Street, Concord
(978) 369–6993
☐ NORTH BRIDGE VISITOR CENTER/MINUTE MAN NHP, MA ⓤ

Bookstore at The Wayside: Home of Authors
399 Lexington Road, Concord
(978) 318–7863
☐ THE WAYSIDE/MINUTE MAN NHP, MA ⓤ
☐ Minute Man NHP/Underground RR Freedom Network ⓤ

17 New Bedford Whaling National Historical Park

New Bedford, Massachusetts
(508) 996–4095
www.nps.gov/nebe

Number of cancellations: One, plus one for the Underground Railroad

Difficulty: Easy

About this site: For much of the nineteenth century, New Bedford served as the leading whaling port in the United States, making it a primary source of whale oil and baleen, products used in virtually every home and business in the country in the early to mid-1800s. This thirty-four-acre, 13-block historical park takes visitors back to the heyday of this thriving community, when New Bedford was known as "the richest city in the world." This area continues to serve those who make their living from the sea. Historic buildings, museums, exhibits, and the working schooner *Ernestina* are some of the park's many offerings.

Stamping tips: There are two visitor centers in this historic area: one managed by the National Park Service, and another called the Waterfront Visitor Center, run by the city of New Bedford. The cancellation is at the National Park Visitor Center, not at the Waterfront Visitor Center.

❗ **Don't miss this!** Plan to spend a day exploring the neighborhoods surrounding the park. Architecture fans will find Federal and Greek Revival structures in abundance, and each has a story to tell. In particular, the Rotch-Jones-Duff House contains especially interesting history, as it was the home of three prominent families in succession from 1834 through 1981. Stroll through the block-wide gardens, tour the furnished period rooms, and get a sense of the prosperity and comfort the residents gained from their connection to the seafaring trades in this remarkable city.

Hours: The visitor center is open daily from 9:00 A.M. to 5:00 P.M. It is closed Thanksgiving, Christmas, and New Year's Day.

Fees: Admission is free to all national park facilities. Some affiliated sites charge admission independently.

New Bedford Whaling Museum: $10.00 for adults, $9.00 for seniors/students, $6.00 for children six to fourteen, free for children five and under.

Rotch-Jones-Duff House and Garden Museum: $5.00 for adults, $4.00 for seniors/students, $2.00 for children three to twelve.

How to get there: From Boston, take Interstate 93 south for 13 miles. Stay right when the highway forks in Braintree; follow the sign for I–93 South/Dedham-Providence. Take exit 4 onto Massachusetts 24 south. This is a left lane exit. Follow MA 24 to exit 12 for Massachusetts 140 south. From MA 140, take exit 2E for Interstate 195 east. Travel on I–195 to exit 15 for downtown New Bedford and Massachusetts 18 south. Turn right at the lights onto Elm Street. The public parking garage is 2 blocks up on the right. The site is at 33 William Street in New Bedford.

Stamping Locations and What the Cancellations Say
New Bedford Whaling National Historical Park Visitor Center

☐ New Bedford Whaling NHP/New Bedford, MA ❶
☐ New Bedford Whaling NHP/Underground RR Freedom Network ❶

🔢 Quinebaug & Shetucket Rivers Valley National Heritage Corridor

Massachusetts NPS Affiliated Area
Salem, Massachusetts (headquarters)
(860) 963–7226
www.nps.gov/qush

Number of cancellations: One

Difficulty: Tricky

About this site: See the entry for this corridor in the Connecticut chapter for a description of the valley and its sights. The Old Sturbridge Village cancellation location marks a northern point in the corridor.

Stamping tips: It is not absolutely necessary for you to pay admission and visit Old Sturbridge Village to get the cancellation, and this 1830s living history museum is not a national park. Some cashiers and managers at this site, however, do feel that Passport stampers should pay the fee and spend time at this site before obtaining the cancellation. It's probably wise to plan to enjoy the village—which is well known for providing an authentic and entertaining historical experience to its guests—just in case you encounter a village staff member who will not release the cancellation without the price of admission.

Two additional cancellations for this National Heritage Corridor are available in Connecticut. See the Connecticut chapter in this guide for details.

❶ Don't miss this! This re-creation of a rural 1830s New England town is the largest of its kind in the Northeast, and it offers the best of the living history museum tradition. You have the option of enjoying demonstrations of nineteenth-century trades and crafts, taking a horse-drawn carriage or sleigh ride (depending on the season), gathering information about heirloom plant varieties in the village's many flower, vegetable, and herb gardens, touring the town with a costumed interpreter, or enjoying the activities around you at your own pace. Old Sturbridge Village also provides shopping and restaurants outside of the village itself, with no admission fee.

Hours: In the winter months, the village is open Wednesday through Sunday, 9:30 A.M. to 4:00 P.M. It is closed Monday and Tuesday, but open on holidays that fall on Monday and on the Tuesday of Presidents' Week in February. From April 1 to the end of October (call for exact dates), the site is open Tuesday through Sunday from 9:30 A.M. to 5:00 P.M. It is closed Mondays, but open on holidays that fall on Monday.

Fees: Winter fees (January–March) are $10.00 for adults and seniors, $5.00 for children three to seventeen, free to children under three. In all other months, fees are $20.00 for adults, $18.00 for seniors over sixty-five, $6.00 for children three to seventeen, and free for children under three. Admission is good for two days within a ten-day period.

How to get there: To reach the Old Sturbridge Village from the Massachusetts Turnpike (Interstate 90), take exit 9, then take the first right onto U.S. Highway 20 west. Continue approximately 0.5 mile, staying in the right lane, and turn right into the entrance, following signs to the village.

Stamping Locations and What the Cancellations Say

Old Sturbridge Village ticket booth

(508) 347–0323

☐ Quinebaug-Shetucket NHC/Old Sturbridge Village ⓿

19 Salem Maritime National Historic Site

Salem, Massachusetts

(978) 740–1650

www.nps.gov/sama

Number of cancellations: Two, plus two for Essex National Heritage Area

Difficulty: Easy

About this site: During the American Revolution, Salem served as a focal point for activity known as privateering, the outfitting of privately owned ships as men-of-war to harass and seize British vessels, thus giving the Americans an advantage they did not have previously over the Royal Navy. Nearly 800 private ships received commissions to undertake this activity, from 200-man privateer vessels to a whaleboat manned by eight fishermen, and this enterprising category of sailors seized upwards of 600 English navy ships. Twelve historic structures along the Salem waterfront tell the story of the men who fought for freedom on the high seas, while sharing details of the famed triangular trade that helped build American prosperity after the colonies gained their independence.

❶ **Don't miss this!** Ranger-led tours are usually worthwhile at all of the parks, as rangers are generally supremely knowledgeable and are often well-practiced speakers and presenters. Salem is one of the places where a ranger-led tour is definitely worth the price of admission. The tour takes you aboard the *Friendship,* a merchant schooner, and through several of the historic homes and buildings along the Salem waterfront. You'll definitely know more about the challenges and very, very simple pleasures of life as a colonist by the end of your tour.

This park also serves as the headquarters for Essex National Heritage Area, an effort by local, state, and national agencies to link thousands of historic places and items under three major subject areas: colonial settlement, maritime trade, and early industrialization in the textile and shoe industries. There's plenty of information here about the Essex National Heritage Area, which will raise your awareness of the linkages between New England national parks and other sites as you travel through the region. See the entry for Essex National Heritage Area in this guide for more information.

Hours: The site is open from 9:00 A.M. to 5:00 P.M. daily. It is closed Thanksgiving, Christmas, and New Year's Day.

Fees: Admission to this park is free. There is a program fee for the ranger-guided tour of the 1797 merchant vessel *Friendship,* the 1819 Custom House, the 1762 Derby House, and the 1672 Narbonne House: $5.00 for adults, and $3.00 for seniors and children.

How to get there: To reach Salem, use Interstate 93 and Interstate 95/Massachusetts 128 or U.S. Highway 1A. Follow signs to Salem. When in Salem, follow signs to the visitor center or the waterfront.

Stamping Locations and What the Cancellations Say

Salem Maritime National Historic Site Orientation Center
193 Derby Street
(978) 740–1660

☐ Salem Maritime National Hist. Site/Salem MA **Ⓤ**

☐ Essex National Heritage Area/Salem, MA **Ⓓ**

Regional visitor center
2 New Liberty Street in downtown Salem
(978) 740–1650

☐ SALEM MARITIME NATIONAL HIST SITE/SALEM, MA **Ⓤ**

☐ Essex National Heritage Area/Salem, MA **Ⓓ**

🔢 Saugus Iron Works National Historic Site

Saugus, Massachusetts
(781) 233–0050
www.nps.gov/sair

Number of cancellations: One, plus one for Essex National Heritage Area

Difficulty: Easy

About this site: Long before American colonists began to think about independence from England, they found ways to turn the natural resources they discovered into materials and products they could use to sustain their way of life. At Saugus, the iron industry found its earliest footing—and the iron works preserved here illustrate just how industrious and innovative the earliest colonists must have been. A blast furnace with 18-foot bellows, forge, and rolling and slitting mill all demonstrate the process of turning iron ore into wrought iron for use in making tools and other items used in other seventeenth-century trades.

Stamping tips: Watch out for the Saugus Iron Works park and visitor center's earlier closing time (4:00 P.M. instead of 5:00 P.M.) from November 1 through March 31.

❶ Don't miss this! The only way to see the seventeenth-century machinery in action is to take the ranger-led tour. Seeing the blast furnace, bellows, forge, and rolling and slitting operation in full, fiery force is well worth the time.

Hours: The park and visitor center are open daily April 1 through October 31 from 9:00 A.M. to 5:00 P.M. From November 1 to March 31, daily hours are 9:00 A.M. to 4:00 P.M. It is closed Thanksgiving, Christmas, and New Year's Day.

Fees: Admission to this park is free.

How to get there: From Interstate 95 northbound or southbound, take exit 43 for Walnut Street. Drive east toward Lynn, and follow the brown National Park Service signs for 3.5 miles to the iron works at 244 Central Street in Saugus.

Stamping Locations and What the Cancellations Say
Saugus Iron Works visitor center

☐ Saugus Iron Works NHS/Saugus, MA **❶**

☐ Essex National Heritage Area/Saugus, MA **❶**

21 Springfield Armory National Historic Site

Springfield, Massachusetts
(413) 734–8551
www.nps.gov/spar

Number of cancellations: One

Difficulty: Easy

About this site: For nearly 200 years, Springfield Armory manufactured the weapons used in every war in America's history; production ended in 1968, when its doors closed for the last time. Turning gun building into a major industry with its innovative manufacturing methods and the high quality of its work, the nation's first armory had a significant impact on American industry. It now houses the largest collection of American military firearms in the world, and exhibits on U.S. innovation in firearms technology.

❶ **Don't miss this!** Beyond the displays of firearms at the armory is the human story of invention and perseverance that helped make the United States the world's strongest military power. Especially fascinating are the tales of the women who manufactured gun parts throughout World War II—the "Rosie the Riveter" workers, referred to here as Women Ordnance Workers (WOWs), whose willingness to take jobs in industry kept munitions flowing to American troops overseas.

Hours: The park is open daily year-round, from 9:00 A.M. to 5:00 P.M. The park is closed New Year's Day, Thanksgiving, and Christmas.

Fees: Admission to this park is free.

How to get there: From the north via Interstate 91, take exit 6 and go to the second traffic light. Turn right onto State Street. Drive to the fifth traffic light and turn left onto Federal Street. Enter the site through the main gate on the left. Once inside the gate, turn left and continue to the museum.

From the south, take I–91 to exit 7. Go to the second traffic light and turn left onto State Street. Follow the directions above to the site.

Stamping Locations and What the Cancellations Say

Springfield Armory information desk

☐ Springfield Armory Nat. Hist. Site/Springfield, MA ❶

New Hampshire

22 Saint-Gaudens National Historic Site

Cornish, New Hampshire
(603) 675–2175
www.nps.gov/saga

Number of cancellations: One

Difficulty: Easy

About this site: You may not recognize the name Augustus Saint-Gaudens, but chances are good that you know this nineteenth- and twentieth-century sculptor's work: the famed "Standing Lincoln" bronze statue in Chicago's Lincoln Park and the monument to General William Sherman at Central Park's Fifty-ninth Street entrance in New York City are two of the exquisitely detailed, strikingly realistic figures he produced. Saint-Gaudens completed monuments, relief portraits, artwork for coins, cameos, and busts in the studio on his estate, now a historic site where visitors can tour his home and view many of his drawings and sculptures. Two of the exhibition galleries, constructed in 1948, stand on the site of one of the artist's original studio spaces, which burned to the ground in 1944.

❶ Don't miss this! You don't need to be an art aficionado to appreciate the quality of Saint-Gaudens's work. The studios and galleries provide plenty of examples of the skill that made Saint-Gaudens one of the most in-demand artists of his day—and so much of this work is still in place in cities and parks across the country that a gallery visit is like a walk down a dearly familiar neighborhood street. The sheer volume of the work he completed in his lifetime is impressive enough; the attention to detail, from the fine lines around Lincoln's eyes to the folds in the uniforms of members of the Fifty-fourth Regiment, inspire awe and respect.

Hours: The site is open Memorial Day weekend through October 31; the buildings and exhibits are open daily from 9:00 A.M. to 4:30 P.M.

From November 1 through the Friday before Memorial Day, only the grounds are open from 8:00 A.M. until dusk. The cancellation is available Monday to Friday in the bookstore during these months.

Fees: $5.00 for adults and children sixteen and older, good for seven days. Children under sixteen are admitted free.

How to get there: The site is 1.5 miles north of the Covered Bridge at Windsor, Vermont, on New Hampshire 12A. Take Interstate 89, exit 20 to West Lebanon, then travel south on NH 12A approximately 12 miles to the site at 139 Saint-Gaudens Road in Cornish.

Stamping Locations and What the Cancellations Say

Bookstore in the Saint-Gaudens visitor center

☐ Saint-Gaudens National Historic Site/Cornish, New Hampshire ⓤ

New York

23 African Burial Ground National Monument

see map on page 84
New York, New York
(212) 637–2039
www.africanburialground.gov/ABG_Main.htm

Number of cancellations: One

Difficulty: Tricky

About this site: This seventeenth- and eighteenth-century cemetery was rediscovered in 1991, when construction of a federal office building began in lower Manhattan at the corner of Duane and Elk Streets. Designated a National Historic Landmark in 1993 and a National Monument in 2006, the site is part of a 6.6-acre site containing the remains of about 15,000 enslaved and free Africans, making this the largest and oldest African cemetery excavated in North America.

❶ Don't miss this! A new visitor center opened in October 2007, including a memorial honoring the enslaved and free Africans who are buried here.

Hours: The visitor center is open Monday through Friday, from 9:00 A.M. to 5:00 P.M., and is closed on weekends and federal holidays. The memorial site is open daily year-round, from 9:00 A.M. to 5:00 P.M., and is closed Thanksgiving, Christmas, and New Year's Day.

Fees: Admission is free.

How to get there: The 4, 5, 6, R, W, J, M, and Z trains (Brooklyn Bridge/City Hall) are 1 block from the site. The A train is 3 blocks away (Chambers Street), the 1 train is 4 blocks away (Chambers Street), and the 2 and 3 trains are 2 blocks away (Park Place).

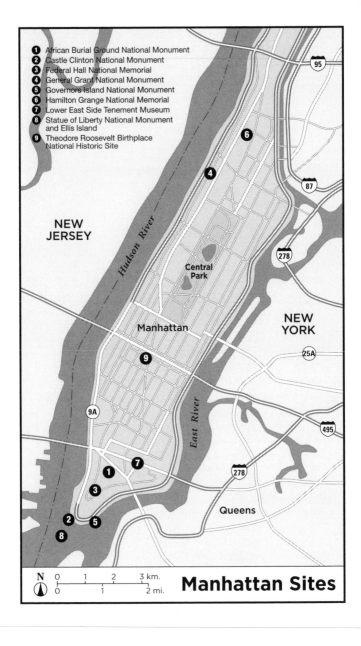

① African Burial Ground National Monument
② Castle Clinton National Monument
③ Federal Hall National Memorial
④ General Grant National Monument
⑤ Governors Island National Monument
⑥ Hamilton Grange National Memorial
⑦ Lower East Side Tenement Museum
⑧ Statue of Liberty National Monument and Ellis Island
⑨ Theodore Roosevelt Birthplace National Historic Site

NEW JERSEY

Hudson River

Central Park

Manhattan

NEW YORK

East River

Queens

N

0   1   2   3 km.
0   1   2 mi.

Manhattan Sites

The A, C, and E trains are 3 blocks away (Chambers/World Trade Center). The M15, M22, and B51 City Hall bus routes all terminate within walking distance, and the M1 and M6 South Ferry routes pass nearby. Ask the driver for the stop closest to Broadway and Duane Street.

Stamping Locations and What the Cancellations Say
African Burial Ground visitor center
☐ African Burial Ground National Monument/New York, NY ◑

24 Castle Clinton National Monument

see map on page 84
New York, New York
(212) 344–7220
www.nps.gov/cacl

Number of cancellations: One

Difficulty: Easy

About this site: The defense of New York Harbor became an important issue in the early 1800s, when conflicts brewed between the new Americans and the still-smarting British over land ownership, as well as England's insistence on capturing American soldiers and forcing them to serve in the British army. This fort—then called the Southwest Battery—was built in 1808–1811, in preparation for the inevitable War of 1812. It never saw combat.

The fort was renamed in honor of DeWitt Clinton, mayor of New York City and later governor of the state of New York. Castle Clinton's military service ended in 1821; it was an entertainment center until 1855, when it was transformed into a landing depot for newcomers to America, the point of entry for more than eight million immigrants. Castle Clinton served as the home of the New York Aquarium from 1896 to 1941, when it was converted to its current use as a museum and ticket office for the Statue of Liberty/Ellis Island ferry.

❶ **Don't miss this!** If you're a military buff, the ranger-led programs are informative, providing more information than you will find in the exhibit area's dioramas. Rangers are skilled in bringing the early days of the War of 1812 to life for visitors.

Hours: The site is open daily from 8:00 A.M. to 5:00 P.M. It is closed Christmas Day.

Fees: Admission to this park is free.

How to get there: From the east, take any bridge or tunnel to Manhattan. Take FDR Drive south to the last exit (exit 1). Take Broad Street to Water Street. Turn left on Water Street to Battery Park.

By bus, take the M1, M6, or M15 bus to Battery Park.

By subway, take the 1 train to South Ferry, 4 or 5 to Bowling Green, or R or W train to Whitehall Street.

You can also take the Staten Island Ferry to Battery Park.

Stamping Locations and What the Cancellations Say

Castle Clinton bookstore

☐ Manhattan Sites Castle Clinton/New York, NY 🕐

25 Eleanor Roosevelt National Historic Site

Hyde Park, New York
(800) 337–8474
www.nps.gov/elro

Number of cancellations: One

Difficulty: Easy

About this site: Of all the nation's first ladies, Eleanor Roosevelt stands out as one of the most significant American women of the twentieth century. Here at Val-Kill, the only home she ever owned personally, the wife of President Franklin Delano Roosevelt could live on her own terms in a home that reflected her style and interests. When away from her work to fight Depression-era poverty and to bolster women's rights, Mrs. Roosevelt entertained visitors from all walks of life and from around the world, exchanging ideas on far-reaching issues including human rights, civil rights, and world peace.

After the president's death in 1945, Eleanor returned to Val-Kill, only to respond the following year to President Truman's call to represent the United States in the United Nations General Assembly. She continued her work to right the wrongs of mankind until her death in 1962.

Stamping tips: The park is not open on Tuesdays and Wednesdays from November through April. While the grounds are open every day year-round, you will not be able to enter the bookstore and get the cancellation while Val-Kill is closed.

🛑 **Don't miss this!** You can't tour the house without a guide—but happily, the guided tour of the house is both informative and charming. Whether or not you are a fan of the venerable Eleanor and her work, the tour guides' tales turn this simple home into the lively center of activity and friendship it must have been while Mrs. Roosevelt resided here. The stories of her unpredictability—and her penchant for double or even tripling the number of dinner guests at a moment's notice—will make you smile, as they bring the first lady's most endearing foibles and greatest accomplishments into the light of day.

Hours: From November through April the site is open Thursday through Monday from 9:00 A.M. to 5:00 P.M. (The last guided tour begins at 4:30 P.M.) It is closed Tuesday and Wednesday. From May through October, the site is open daily from 9:00 A.M. to 5:00 P.M.

The grounds are open daily year-round until sunset, and are closed Thanksgiving Day, Christmas, and New Year's Day.

Fees: Entrance to the park grounds is free.

The tour of Val-Kill costs $8.00 for adults, and is free for children fifteen and under. All visitors (including children) must have a tour ticket to join a guided tour. Access to Val-Kill is by guided tour only. Reservations are recommended.

How to get there: From the New York State Thruway (Interstate 87), take exit 18/New Paltz. Follow New York 299 east to U.S. Highway 9W. Follow US 9W south to the Mid-Hudson Bridge. Cross the bridge and exit onto U.S. Highway 9 northbound for Hyde Park.

From New York City, take the Henry Hudson Parkway/New York 9A north to Sawmill River Parkway. Follow the Sawmill River Parkway north to the Taconic State Parkway northbound. Exit at New York 55 west for Poughkeepsie, and follow that to US 9 north into Hyde Park.

Stamping Locations and What the Cancellations Say

Eleanor Roosevelt NHS bookstore

4097 Post Road, Hyde Park

☐ Eleanor Roosevelt NHS/Hyde Park, NY 🛑

New York NPS Affiliated Area
Buffalo to Albany, New York
(518) 237–7000
www.nps.gov/erie

Number of cancellations: Five, plus cancellations for five other national park sites, and one for the Underground Railroad

Difficulty: Challenging

About this site: When it opened in 1825, the Erie Canal quickly became the most successful and influential waterway in North America, linking the cities of upstate New York and creating the first all-water route from the Atlantic Ocean to the Great Lakes.

While the original canal was 363 miles long, this National Heritage Corridor connects 524 miles of working waterway, including the Erie, Cayuga-Seneca, Oswego, and Champlain Canals. Many canals across the country tried to emulate the Erie's success, but this canal remains the leader to this day—the canal that made New York City the nation's strongest seaport, by bringing people, ideas, and goods from all over the world into the American interior and taking raw, refined, and milled materials from middle America to ships in New York Harbor, where they became the high-quality exports that fueled our nation's growth.

Stamping tips: Be sure to ask for the cancellations at each of the sites. As four of these sites are national parks in their own right, each is a two- or three-cancellation stop.

A development plan for more sites along the corridor is reaching completion—look for more information at www.nps.gov/erie.

❗ **Don't miss this!** More than 200 miles of the Erie Canal towpath are maintained, ready for walking, biking, or in-line skating (on the paved portions) for an hour, a day, or even a cross-state marathon. This straight, mostly level, easy cycling path follows the canal across New York state, where mules once towed barges, as the traditional folk song goes, "filled with lumber, coal, and hay," from Albany to Buffalo.

You'll pass through quiet residential areas, quaint towns, and long stretches of undeveloped woods and farmland, with only an occasional intersection with motorized traffic. If you want to see upstate New York in all of its luscious, green, summer glory—or in the fiery reds and golds of a north Atlantic autumn—there's no better method than a leisurely bike ride or walk along this historic path. Plus, you'll see working locks, remains of old canal barges and ships, and plenty of pleasure boats as they putt-putt past (there's a law against wakes on the canal, so boats travel at a slow, relaxed pace).

Hours: The Erie Canalway visitor center in Waterford is open daily from Memorial Day to Labor Day from 10:00 A.M. to 5:00 P.M. From Labor Day to Columbus Day, it is open Saturday and Sunday from 10:00 A.M. to 5:00 P.M. It is closed from Columbus Day to Memorial Day.

Most towpath sections of the Erie Canalway are open year-round from dawn until dusk. The canal is drained every fall (around November 15) and refilled in the spring (early May), so it is closed to boat traffic during the winter. For information on lock hours of operation, contact the New York State Canal Corporation at www.canals.state.ny.us.

For hours at each of the national park sites that have Erie Canalway cancellations, see their listings in this book.

Fees: There are no admission fees to the Erie Canalway and most of the towpath sections. There are fees for boating through the locks, and private and non-profit historic sites may charge admission or accept donations for special events and programs.

How to get there: The Erie Canalway passes through the middle of upstate New York from Buffalo to Albany. For directions to specific sites and attractions along its 524-mile route, go to www.ptny.org/canalway/index.shtml. You may also check out the link on the National Park Service Web site to www.eriecanalway.org, which includes maps and other resources.

To reach **Fort Stanwix,** take the New York State Thruway (Interstate 90) to exit 32 (Westmoreland), and follow the signs to the monument in Rome, New York.

To reach the **Theodore Roosevelt Inaugural site** in Buffalo, take I-90 west to exit 51. Take the exit onto New York 33 west (Kensington Expressway), and head into the downtown area. Continue west for 6.5 miles on NY 33. Take the Goodell Street exit and get into the center lane of Goodell. Follow the signs to Delaware Avenue. At Main Street, continue to follow the signs to Delaware Avenue, veer left around Saint Louis Church, and go west on Edward Street. To reach the site's free parking lot, turn right at the first street, Franklin, and travel 2⅗ blocks north. The lot entrance is on the left and marked by a brown-and-white National Park Service sign. The park site is at 641 Delaware Avenue.

To reach the Theodore Roosevelt Inaugural site from the south or west, take I–90 to exit 53 for Interstate 190 north. Take I–190, and go west for 5.5 miles to exit 8 for Niagara Street. Turn left on Niagara Street, and go northwest for 0.7 mile to Porter Avenue. Turn left onto Porter Avenue, and go northeast to Symphony Circle. Pass through Symphony Circle (Porter becomes North Street). Go east for 0.5 mile to Delaware Avenue. Turn right onto Delaware Avenue. The site is on your left.

Saratoga National Historical Park is located 40 miles north of Albany and 15 miles southeast of Saratoga Springs at 648 New York 32 in Stillwater. From Montreal and points north, take Interstate 87 to exit 14, and follow New York 29 east to Schuylerville, where the Schuyler House (at the south end of town) and the Saratoga Monument are located. At the T intersection with U.S. Highway 4, turn right. The battlefield entrance is 8 miles south on US 4.

To reach Saratoga National Historical Park from Albany and points south, follow I–87 to exit 12. Turn right off the exit; you will be on New York 67. After the first light, move into the left lane (turning lane). At the second light, turn left onto U.S. Highway 9 northbound. Turn right on New York 9P, and proceed to Saratoga Lake. Turn right on NY 32. Turn left, and follow the signs to the park entrance at 648 NY 32.

To reach **Women's Rights National Historical Park** from the New York State Thruway (I–90), take exit 41 for New York 414. Turn right onto NY 414 after exiting the tolls. Follow NY 414 for approximately 4 miles. At the intersections of NY 414 and New York 5/U.S. Highway 20 (the same road at this point), turn left onto NY 5/US 20. Follow this road approximately 1.5 miles into the village of Seneca Falls. The visitor center is on the left at 136 Fall Street.

Stamping Locations and What the Cancellations Say

Stamping locations are listed as you would find them if traveling from Buffalo east to Stillwater.

Theodore Roosevelt Inaugural National Historic Site Visitor Center
641 Delaware Avenue, Buffalo
(716) 884–0095
- [ ] Erie Canalway NHC/Buffalo, NY ⓤ
- [ ] Theodore Roosevelt Inaugural NHS/Buffalo, NY ⓤ

Women's Rights National Historical Park Visitor Center
136 Fall Street, Seneca Falls
(315) 568–2991
- [ ] Erie Canalway NHC/Seneca Falls, NY ⓤ
- [ ] Women's Rights Nat'l Historical Park/Seneca Falls, NY ⓤ
- [ ] Women's Rights NHP/Underground RR Freedom Network ⓤ

Fort Stanwix National Monument bookstore
112 E Park Street, Rome
(315) 338–7730
- [ ] Erie Canalway NHC/Rome, NY ⓤ
- [ ] Fort Stanwix National Monument/Rome, NY ⓤ
- [ ] North Country National Scenic Trail/New York ⓓ

Erie Canalway National Heritage Corridor Visitor Center
Peebles Island State Park, Waterford
(518) 237–7000
- [ ] Erie Canalway NHC/Waterford, NY ⓤ

Saratoga National Historical Park Visitor Center
648 NY 32, Stillwater
(518) 664–9821
- [ ] Erie Canalway NHC/Stillwater, NY ⓤ
- [ ] Saratoga Nat'l Historical Park/Stillwater, NY ⓤ

27 Federal Hall National Memorial

see map on page 84
New York, New York
(212) 825–6872
www.nps.gov/feha

Number of cancellations: One

Difficulty: Easy

About this site: George Washington was sworn in as the first president of the United States here on April 30, 1789. If that fact alone isn't attractive enough, consider these: This former New York City Hall site served as the national capitol for the United States' first year as an independent nation. The Stamp Act Congress, which organized protests against "taxation without representation," met here in 1765. Newspaper publisher John Peter Zenger was tried and acquitted here for exposing government corruption in his paper, scoring the first major victory for freedom of the press. The First Congress met here and wrote the Bill of Rights, before the nation's capitol moved to Philadelphia in 1790.

All of this being said, the building that stands at 26 Wall Street today is not the original New York City Hall. This impressive structure was built in 1842, and has served as the Customs House and as the Federal Reserve—at one time, millions of dollars' worth of precious metals sat in the building's basement vaults.

Stamping tips: Federal Hall is open Monday through Friday, but not on weekends.

This is a federal government building, complete with metal detectors and security personnel, so leave your pocketknife in your hotel room or car, or risk confiscation. Some guards are willing to hold your forbidden item at the front desk while you visit the site, but some are not, and you may be turned away.

❶ Don't miss this! Federal Hall is a short stop with interesting displays (including the Bible upon which Washington placed his hand during his inauguration) and a colorful history—but its most intriguing feature is its proximity to Ground Zero, the former site of the World Trade Center and the focal point of the September 11, 2001, terrorist attacks. While construction progresses on the new 1,776-foot Freedom Tower that will replace most of the center, visitors can take a self-guided tour around the perimeter of the site, where photos and displays tell the story of the attack, the rescue effort, and the plan to rebuild.

For a more in-depth exploration, take advantage of a truly extraordinary opportunity to experience history through the eyes of its participants by touring the site with a volunteer who has a personal connection to the events that happened here. Tour leaders lost loved ones, worked in the World Trade Center and survived the attack, or came to help with the rescue effort, and their stories focus on the courage and hope that arose out of tragedy. Each tour begins at 120 Liberty Street, the site of the organization's Tribute Center, and lasts approximately one hour. Tours leave daily at 1:00 P.M., and twice daily on weekends at noon and 2:00 P.M. Fees for tours are $10.00 per person; children under twelve are admitted free. For reservations, visit www.telecharge .com, click on "Other Events," then on "Tribute Center Walking Tour."

Hours: Federal Hall is open from 9:00 A.M. to 5:00 P.M. Monday through Friday. The park is closed on all national holidays.

Fees: Admission to this park is free.

How to get there: Driving in downtown Manhattan is not for the faint of heart, and parking is very limited and expensive (as much as $12.00 to $20.00 for a short stop).

To reach the site via subway, take the 2 and 3 subway trains, which stop at Wall and William Streets, one block east of Federal Hall. The 4 and 5 subway trains stop at Wall Street and Broadway, one block west of Federal Hall. The J, M, and Z subway trains stop at Wall and Broad Streets Monday through Friday. See www.mta.info for schedules and information.

Stamping Locations and What the Cancellations Say

Federal Hall information desk

26 Wall Street

☐ FEDERAL HALL N MEM/NEW YORK, NY ⓤ

🟦28 Fire Island National Seashore

Patchogue, New York
(631) 289–4810
www.nps.gov/fiis

Number of cancellations: Seven

Difficulty: Heroic

About this site: Preservation of open space is not a concept usually associated with the New York City metropolitan area, but Fire
Island became a national seashore for exactly this purpose—to
keep 26 miles of barrier islands containing unspoiled beach and
wilderness from succumbing to encroaching urban development.

While seventeen preexisting communities remain within the
bounds of the park, the island has no paved roads beyond those
that reach South Point County Park on one end and Robert Moses
State Park on the other, so this is the perfect place to escape the
crush of city and suburban congestion and noise. Access to most
of Fire Island National Seashore is by ferry, while miles of trails
and boardwalks lead through sand dunes and salt marshes,
offering panoramic views of minimally populated beaches and
opportunities for wildlife viewing. Canoeing, boating, beachcombing, swimming, and fishing are some of the park's most
popular activities.

Stamping tips: Forget about getting all seven cancellations at
this park in one day! While it may be physically possible, the
sheer amount of driving, walking, and ferry riding required would
turn your day at Fire Island into a logistical nightmare. By all
means, take your time—at least two days, and maybe three if you
do some beachcombing, swimming, and hiking. Make the most
of a wilderness getaway within shouting distance of the nation's
largest metropolis.

Cancellation stamp collecting reaches a dizzying level of
complexity because two cancellations—Sailors Haven and Watch
Hill—reside at sites accessible only by ferry, private boat, or by
foot, and the hike between them is nearly 7 miles each way.
Probably the most effective (if expensive) method for collecting
these two cancellations is to take the ferry from the mainland to
one of the sites, and then use Fire Island's water taxi system
to travel between them (for full details on the water taxi, visit
www.fireislandwatertaxi.com). The water taxi service divides the

island into eight zones, and its rides are priced according to the number of zones you cross; a taxi ride from Sailors Haven to Watch Hill crosses four zones, for a fare of $12.00 per person. The return trip is another $12.00.

Another cancellation stamp collecting option is to drive to the Fire Island Lighthouse Visitor Center, where you'll get your first cancellation. Take the water taxi to Sailors Haven ($14.00 per person), then on to Watch Hill ($12.00 per person). Relax and enjoy the water taxi ride from Watch Hill all the way back to Fire Island Lighthouse, because you've paid well for the privilege at the startling price of $22.00 per person. It'll cost $48.00 per person to get these three cancellations, plus $10.00 per vehicle to park, but you've also spent an especially pleasant and memorable day exploring and cruising the length of the national seashore. (All fares are in 2007 dollars.)

If you'd rather skip the pricey water taxi, here's a suggested itinerary for Fire Island cancellation stamp collecting:

Drive to Robert Moses State Park. Go south on the Robert Moses Causeway, crossing Captree Island, to a point near the Fire Island Coast Guard Station. Continue around the circle at the water tower, then bear right and drive east toward the Fire Island Lighthouse, one of the tallest on the eastern seaboard. The walk to the top is 192 steps with several landings, and lighthouse personnel conduct special sunset programs on some days.

Return to the mainland, and take New York 27 to Lakeland Avenue in Sayville. Follow this to Railroad Avenue, then to Main Street (New York 27A), and turn left. Bear right at the Y onto Middle Road. Turn right on Foster Avenue to reach the Sailors Haven Ferry Terminal. Check at www.sayvilleferry.com/sf.htm for ferry schedules; tickets are $19.00 round-trip for adults and $9.00 for children under twelve. After the half-hour ferry ride, get the cancellation at the Sailors Haven Visitor Center, walk the Sunken Forest boardwalk or stroll to the beach, and ride the ferry back to the mainland.

Return to NY 27A, and go right (east) to Patchogue. Turn right on West Avenue, pass the Watch Hill Ferry Terminal, and continue down the road to the Fire Island National Seashore Park Headquarters, where you'll find the Patchogue, New York, cancellation. Collect the cancellation, chat with the staff, and then go north on West Avenue to the ferry terminal. Take the

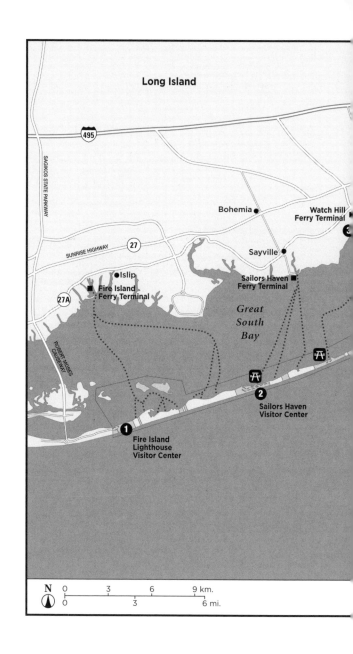

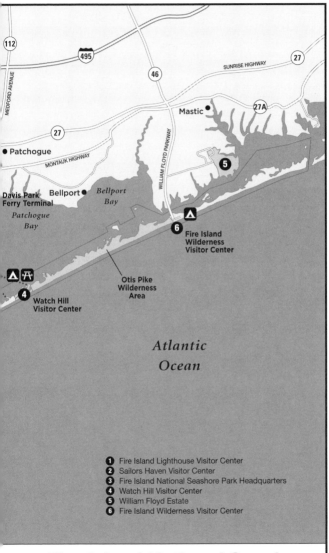

112

495

27 SUNRISE HIGHWAY 27

MEDFORD AVENUE

46

27A

Mastic •

27

● Patchogue

WILLIAM FLOYD PARKWAY

MONTAUK HIGHWAY

5

Davis Park
Ferry Terminal

Bellport ● *Bellport Bay*

Patchogue Bay

6 Fire Island
Wilderness
Visitor Center

4 Watch Hill
Visitor Center

Otis Pike
Wilderness
Area

Atlantic Ocean

1 Fire Island Lighthouse Visitor Center
2 Sailors Haven Visitor Center
3 Fire Island National Seashore Park Headquarters
4 Watch Hill Visitor Center
5 William Floyd Estate
6 Fire Island Wilderness Visitor Center

Fire Island National Seashore

Watch Hill Ferry (631–475–1665 or www.davisparkferry.com/wh. shtml) to the Watch Hill Visitor Center. Collect the cancellation, enjoy the center and self-guided nature trail, and return by ferry to Patchogue.

If time permits and the William Floyd Estate is open, turn east on NY 27A, drive to New York 46, and turn right on NY 46/ William Floyd Parkway. From the Floyd Parkway, turn left onto Neighborhood Road, then left at Park Drive. The entrance is on your right. At the Old Manor House, you'll find the William Floyd cancellation.

As you leave the estate grounds, turn left onto Washington Avenue, then left onto Mastic Beach Road, and right on Neighborhood Road. Return to the Floyd Parkway, and turn left to reach the Fire Island Wilderness Visitor Center, where the last two cancellations are waiting for you.

As if the cancellations' wide distribution and limited accessibility were not enough to make Passport enthusiasts yank out their own hair, most of Fire Island is closed from November to the beginning of May, and the ferry services do not run during the winter.

❶ Don't miss this! Now that you've left the car behind to explore Sailors Haven and Watch Hill, it's time for a pleasant, cool walk—and Sunken Forest, a 250-year-old stand of holly, sassafras, and other maritime species, provides a welcome respite from the hot sun. A forest is just about the last thing you'd expect to find on a barrier island, where inhospitable weather usually prohibits such old growth—but a second set of sand dunes at Sailors Haven protects this patch, keeping it safe from high winds and salt spray. An easy 1.5-mile boardwalk meanders through this forest and into the swale zone between the dunes, where you can see just how the double dunes contribute to the survival of this complex ecosystem.

William Floyd's name may not be familiar to you, but his signature appears on the Declaration of Independence. This Revolutionary War general was born in 1734 in the plantation house at the northeast end of the seashore, and the surrounding grounds form a well-maintained wildlife refuge. If eighteenth-century architecture is your passion, the tour will satisfy your curiosity—but if you walk the grounds, be sure to roll down your sleeves and wear long pants, socks, and shoes, as ticks are particularly pernicious.

Hours: Sailors Haven Visitor Center is open from mid-May to mid-June from 10:00 A.M. to 1:00 P.M. Monday to Friday, and from 10:00 A.M. to 2:30 P.M. on Saturday and Sunday. From mid-June to Labor Day, it is open daily from 9:30 A.M. to 3:30 P.M. From Labor Day to mid-October, it is open on weekends and holidays that fall on Monday from 11:00 A.M. to 2:30 P.M.

Watch Hill Visitor Center is open from mid-May to mid-June on weekends from 9:00 A.M. to 5:00 P.M. From mid-June to Labor Day, it is open daily from 9:00 A.M. to 5:00 P.M. From Labor Day to mid-October, it is open Friday to Sunday and on holidays that fall on Monday from 9:00 A.M. to 5:00 P.M.

Fire Island Lighthouse Visitor Center is open daily from July 1 to Labor Day from 9:30 A.M. to 5:30 P.M. From Labor Day to mid-December, it is open daily from 9:30 A.M. to 5:00 P.M. eastern daylight time/4:00 P.M. eastern standard time. From January 1 to mid-March, it is open daily from noon to 4:00 P.M. From April 1 through June 30, it is open daily from 9:30 A.M. to 5:00 P.M.

Fire Island National Seashore headquarters in Patchogue is open Monday to Friday year-round, from 9:00 A.M. to 4:30 P.M. It is closed on all federal holidays.

William Floyd Estate is open from the end of May to October 31, from Friday to Sunday and on holidays that fall on Monday, from 11:00 A.M. to 4:30 P.M.

Fire Island Wilderness Visitor Center is open from May 1 to mid-June on weekends from 9:00 A.M. to 4:00 P.M. From mid-June to December 31, it is open Wednesday to Sunday from 9:00 A.M. to 4:00 P.M. The center is closed from January 1 through April 30.

Fees: Admission to this park is free. However, the parking lots near the lighthouse, the Sayville ferry terminal, and the Wilderness Visitor Center charge $8.00 to $10.00 for parking.

How to get there: From the Long Island Expressway (LIE/Interstate 495), take exit 53 for the Sagikos State Parkway to get to the Fire Island Lighthouse. Go south on the parkway until it becomes the Robert Moses Causeway, which crosses Oyster Bay and Captree Island before ending at the Fire Island Coast Guard Station in Robert Moses State Park. Turn left, and drive east to the Fire Island Lighthouse Visitor Center.

NOTE: The road ends at the visitor center. Much of this park is accessible only by ferry; see Stamping tips for more information and directions to other sites.

Stamping Locations and What the Cancellations Say

Fire Island Lighthouse Visitor Center
(631) 661–4876
Located down the boardwalk from the Robert Moses State Park parking lot

☐ Fire Island National Seashore/Lighthouse ⓞ

Sailors Haven Visitor Center
(631) 597–6183
Accessible by Sayville Ferry, private boat, or on foot. Open seasonally.

☐ Fire Island National Seashore/Sailors Haven ⓞ

Fire Island National Seashore Park Headquarters
Patchogue
(631) 687–4750

☐ Fire Island National Seashore/Long Island, NY ⓞ

Watch Hill Visitor Center
(631) 597–6455
Accessible only by private boat, foot, and Watch Hill Ferry out of Patchogue. Open seasonally.

☐ Fire Island National Seashore/Watch Hill ⓞ

William Floyd Estate
(631) 399–2030

☐ Fire Island National Seashore/William Floyd Estate ⓞ

Fire Island Wilderness Visitor Center
(631) 281–3010
The Long Island cancellation is on the first floor; the Wilderness cancellation is on the second floor.

☐ Fire Island National Seashore/Long Island, NY ⓞ

☐ Fire Island National Seashore/Wilderness ⓞ

29 Fort Stanwix National Monument

Rome, New York
(315) 336–2090
www.nps.gov/fost

Number of cancellations: One, plus cancellations for Erie Canalway National Heritage Corridor and North Country National Scenic Trail

Difficulty: Easy

About this site: This scrupulously thorough 1970s reproduction of the original Fort Stanwix (built in 1758) serves as a reminder of a pivotal Revolutionary War battle in 1777, when American soldiers stood their ground and refused to surrender to Lieutenant Colonel Barry St. Leger, leader of the British Western invasion from Canada. Clever maneuvering by American commanders—including Benedict Arnold, who fooled St. Leger into believing the American forces were much stronger than they were—led St. Leger and his demoralized troops to retreat to Montreal,

Two important treaties with Native Americans also had their origins at Fort Stanwix. The first, enacted in 1784 between British troops and the Iroquois tribes, established a new boundary line between British and Iroquois lands, essentially ceding the Iroquois' ownership of Kentucky to the Europeans. While the treaty was meant to stave off additional violence, it served to incite more anger and raids, culminating years later along the Ohio River in the Dunmore War. A 1784 treaty surrendered Iroquois claims to land in Pennsylvania and Ohio, leading to even more violence and delaying final resolution until the Ohio Indian wars.

Don't miss this! The new Marinus Willett Collections Management and Education Center opened in July 2005, providing much greater access to the fort's collection of 485,000 artifacts, many of which were found during the twentieth-century archeological excavation of the original fort site. The exhibits work to help visitors see the Revolutionary War era in upstate New York through the eyes of those who lived, worked, and defended their liberty here, while housing a collection that, until now, maintained precarious residency in a tunnel under the fort.

Hours: The park is open daily year-round, from 9:00 A.M. to 5:00 P.M. It is closed Thanksgiving and Christmas, and New Year's Day. The fort is open daily from April 1 to December 31, from

9:00 A.M. to 4:45 P.M. It is closed on Thanksgiving, Christmas, and from January 1 to March 31.

Fees: Admission to this park is free.

How to get there: Take the New York State Thruway (Interstate 90) to exit 32 (Westmoreland), and follow the signs to the monument.

Stamping Locations and What the Cancellations Say

Fort Stanwix Visitor Center bookstore

112 East Park Street, Rome

☐ Fort Stanwix National Monument/Rome, NY ❶

☐ North Country National Scenic Trail/New York ❶

☐ Erie Canalway NHC/Rome, NY ❶

③⓪ Gateway National Recreation Area

Staten Island, New York
(718) 354–4606
www.nps.gov/gate

Number of cancellations: Seven, including the cancellation in Sandy Hook, New Jersey, plus a cancellation for the New Jersey Coastal Heritage Trail Route

Difficulty: Challenging

About this site: What's unusual about Gateway is not its geologic or natural significance, but the fact that it exists at all in the most developed urban area in the country. As one of the nation's few urban national parks, Gateway offers visitors from a natural getaway complete with pristine beaches and wildlife refuges, as well as historic military sites, music and other cultural events, sailing, surfing, and organized sports.

Visitors can see New York's first municipal airport at Floyd Bennett Field, the military fortifications at Fort Tilden, Miller Field, Fort Wadsworth, and Fort Hancock, and the thriving ecosystem that survives despite encroaching development around Jamaica Bay and New York Harbor. These 26,000 acres provide a haven from city life for more than seven million people every year.

Stamping tips: Note that three of the cancellation locations—Fort Wadsworth, Miller Field, and Great Kills—are not open daily. If you want to get all six New York Gateway cancellations in one day, that day will need to be a Friday, Saturday, or Sunday, when all six sites are open for business.

Cancellation collecting at Gateway follows a great circular route through three New York boroughs, so if you want to get all the cancellations in one day, be prepared to grapple with Big Apple traffic that will slow your progress. Gateway is the fourth-most-visited national park, with more than eight million guests annually, so even the off-season can be congested. With its beaches, multiple concert series, numerous opportunities for outdoor sports and recreation, and special events featuring the New York Philharmonic, Metropolitan Opera, and the New York City Marathon, there aren't many "down days" at Gateway.

The third unit of the park is in New Jersey, a significant distance from the next closest unit in Staten Island (compounded by metropolitan traffic), so before you embark on your stamping cycle, seriously consider splitting your Gateway visit into two days. You'll have more opportunity to admire the scenery, take in a concert, explore a bike trail, or scan the wildlife refuge for interesting birds and animals if you acknowledge the stamping challenge in advance.

Leaving Sandy Hook in New Jersey for the next day, one suggested route follows for gathering as many cancellations as you can in one day:

Begin at the Ryan Visitor Center at Floyd Bennett Field, on the Brooklyn side of the park. Travel down Flatbush Avenue to the center, secure the cancellation, and continue south on Flatbush across the Gil Hodges Bridge to the park's Breezy Point District. As you come off the bridge, bear right toward Breezy Point, make the first left into Fort Tilden, and follow the signs to the Visitor Contact Station in Building 1.

Get the cancellation, and then return to and pass the entrance to the Gil Hodges Bridge. Follow Beach Channel Drive to the Veterans Memorial Bridge, which will cross Jamaica Bay on the left. Cross the bay to the cluster of islands that make up the Jamaica Bay Wildlife Refuge, and stop at the visitor center to obtain the refuge cancellation.

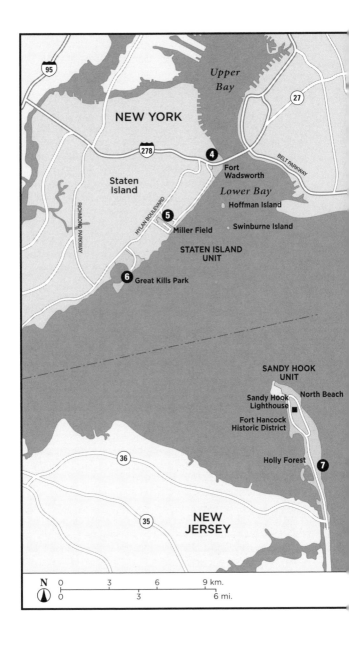

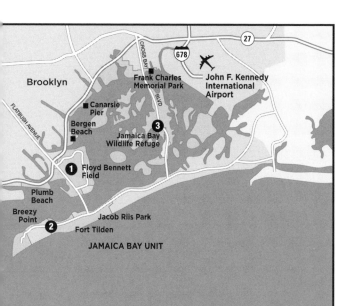

Brooklyn

FLATBUSH AVENUE

Canarsie Pier

Bergen Beach

① Floyd Bennett Field

Plumb Beach

Breezy Point

②

Jacob Riis Park

Fort Tilden

JAMAICA BAY UNIT

CROSS BAY BLVD

678

27

Frank Charles Memorial Park

John F. Kennedy International Airport

③ Jamaica Bay Wildlife Refuge

Atlantic Ocean

① Ryan Visitor Center, Floyd Bennett Field
② Fort Tilden Visitor Contact Station
③ Jamaica Bay Wildlife Refuge Visitor Center
④ Fort Wadsworth Visitor Center
⑤ Miller Field Ranger Station
⑥ Great Kills Park Ranger Station
⑦ Sandy Hook Visitor Center

Gateway National Recreation Area

Having collected all the cancellations in Brooklyn and Queens, proceed back to the mainland by driving north across the Joseph P. Addabbo Bridge to Cross Bay Boulevard. Turn left onto Shore (Belt) Parkway, and follow it across the Verrazano Narrows Bridge onto Staten Island. You'll pass the Canarsie Pier Visitor Center, the one center in Gateway that does not have a Passport cancellation. You may want to make a quick stop just to check; it seems likely that a cancellation will pop up at Canarsie Pier one day.

At the Staten Island end of the Verrazano Narrows Bridge, follow signs to Fort Wadsworth. Collect your fourth cancellation at this site (note that this location is closed on Monday and Tuesday). From Fort Wadsworth, take Interstate 278 to Hylan Boulevard, which takes you southwest to New Dorp Lane. Turn east onto New Dorp and proceed to the Miller Field Ranger Station for your next cancellation (also not available on Monday and Tuesday).

Return to Hylan Boulevard, turn left, and follow Hylan to Great Kills Park. The cancellation is at the Great Kills Ranger Station. This is your sixth and last Gateway Passport cancellation in New York State.

If you want to proceed to Sandy Hook in New Jersey immediately, return to Hylan Boulevard; turn left and follow Hylan to the Richmond Parkway. At the junction of Richmond and I–278, take I–278 to the mainland, take Interstate 95 south, and continue to the Garden State Parkway. Take the parkway south to New Jersey 36, the exit for Sandy Hook; NJ 36 leads to Gateway's New Jersey unit.

Don't miss this! The Jamaica Bay Wildlife Refuge is one of the most important urban wildlife refuges in the United States, with more than 330 bird species found here over the years. If you have never seen hundreds of tiny shorebirds (those little "peeps" that run back and forth along the beach) in one place, or heard the sheer decibel power of tens of thousands of ducks and geese as they flock during their annual migration, Jamaica Bay is one of the few places in the country where you can witness these *National Geographic*–style moments.

This refuge has become a stopping point for monarch butterfly migration as well, one of the most astonishing natural phenomena on our planet. Thousands of these delicate creatures rest on milkweed and other familiar plants in the park while they store up strength to move ever onward.

Linger in the refuge if you can, and stand still in a wild place for a little while... and you will see some of the hidden creatures with which we share our world.

Hours: Ryan Visitor Center at Floyd Bennett Field is open daily from 8:30 A.M. to 5:00 P.M.

Fort Tilden Visitor Contact Station is open daily from 9:00 A.M. to 4:00 P.M.

Jamaica Bay Wildlife Refuge Visitor Center is open daily from 8:30 A.M. to 5:00 P.M.

Fort Wadsworth Visitor Center is open from 10:00 A.M. to 5:00 P.M. Wednesday to Sunday. It is closed Monday and Tuesday.

Miller Field Ranger Station is open Wednesday to Sunday from 8:30 A.M. to 5:00 P.M. It is closed Monday and Tuesday.

Great Kills Park Ranger Station is open from 9:00 A.M. to 4:30 P.M. Friday to Monday; it is closed Thanksgiving, Christmas, and New Year's Day.

Fees: Admission to this park is free. Parking fees are in effect in summer at Jacob Riis Park and Sandy Hook; call for current rates.

How to get there: The park has two units in New York State: Brooklyn/Queens and Staten Island. A third unit, Sandy Hook, is in New Jersey.

To reach **Floyd Bennett Field** (Jamaica Bay Unit), follow the Belt Parkway to exit 11S. Take Flatbush Avenue south to the main entrance.

To reach the **Jamaica Bay Wildlife Refuge** (Jamaica Bay Unit), follow the Belt Parkway to exit 17/Cross Bay Boulevard. Proceed south on Cross Bay Boulevard across the north Channel Bridge. The refuge visitor center is about 1 mile past the bridge, at the traffic light.

To reach **Jacob Riis Park/Fort Tilden** (Jamaica Bay Unit), follow the Belt Parkway to exit 11S, then take Flatbush Avenue south across the Marine Parkway Bridge to the park. Alternatively, take Woodhaven Boulevard to Cross Bay Boulevard, then go west on Beach Channel Drive to the park.

To reach **Fort Wadsworth** (Staten Island Unit) from Brooklyn, take the lower level of the Verrazano Narrows Bridge/I–278. Beyond the toll, take the Bay Street exit. Turn left at the light, and proceed to Bay Street and the park entrance.

To reach **Miller Field** from Fort Wadsworth, return to the Staten Island Expressway (I–278), and take the Hylan Boulevard exit. Proceed south on Hylan Boulevard and turn east on New Dorp Lane to Miller Field.

To reach **Great Kills Park** from Miller Field, go south on Hylan Boulevard to the Great Kills Park entrance.

To reach **Sandy Hook** in New Jersey, take the Garden State Parkway to exit 117, then follow NJ 36 east for 12 miles to the park entrance.

Stamping Locations and What the Cancellations Say

Ryan Visitor Center
Floyd Bennett Field
(718) 338–3799
☐ Floyd Bennett Field/Gateway National Recreation Area ⓤ

Fort Tilden Visitor Contact Station
(718) 318–4300
☐ Gateway National Recreation Area/Breezy Point, Fort Tilden, NY ⓤ

Jamaica Bay Wildlife Refuge Visitor Center
(718) 318–4340
☐ Gateway NRA–Wildlife Refuge District/Queens, NY ⓤ

Fort Wadsworth Visitor Center
(718) 354–4500
☐ Gateway Nat'l Recreation Area/Ft. Wadsworth ⓤ

Miller Field Ranger Station
(718) 351–6970
☐ Gateway NRA–Miller Field/Staten Island, NY ⓤ

Great Kills Park Ranger Station
(718) 987–6790
☐ Gateway NRA–Great Kills Park/Staten Island, NY ⓤ

Sandy Hook Visitor Center
☐ Gateway Nat'l Rec. Area–Sandy Hook/Highlands, NJ ⓤ
☐ New Jersey Coastal Heritage Trail Route (no bottom text) ⓓ

see map on page 84
New York, New York
(212) 666–1640
www.nps.gov/gegr

Number of cancellations: One

Difficulty: Easy

About this site: The eighteenth president of the United States, General Ulysses S. Grant, is entombed here with his wife, first lady Julia Dent Grant. The venerable general led the Union to victory in the Civil War, and went on to succeed Andrew Johnson as president.

During his two terms in office, Grant signed into law the Civil Rights Act of 1875, which gave African Americans the right to equal treatment with whites in public places; he also named Yellowstone as the first national park on March 1, 1872. While Grant was laid to rest in New York City in August 1885, overwhelmingly positive public opinion demanded that this much-loved president be honored with the largest and most permanent monument money could buy—and to this end, more than 90,000 people contributed cash for its construction. Grant was entombed in April 1897, with more than one million people attending to honor his memory.

Stamping tips: If you're using public transportation to stamp your way through New York City, the nearest subway will let you off about six blocks from the monument. There is limited parking—more than you'll find at most other Manhattan national park sites, so consider driving and making this a stop on your way north, before you visit Saint Paul's Church in Mount Vernon. Luckily, the Grant memorial is open daily year-round, so it will fit into whatever schedule you establish.

❶ **Don't miss this!** You don't need much time to enjoy the memorial, so take a few minutes to examine the mosaics around the inside. You'll see Grant at his most glorious, battling armies at Vicksburg and Chattanooga, and accepting Robert E. Lee's surrender at Appomattox.

Hours: The site is open year-round from 9:00 A.M. to 5:00 P.M. It is closed Thanksgiving, Christmas, and New Year's Day.

Fees: Admission to this park is free.

How to get there: General Grant National Memorial is located at 122nd Street and Riverside Drive in Manhattan.

By car: From the north, use the George Washington Bridge/Interstate 95/Cross Bronx Expressway, or Interstate 87/Major Deegan Expressway. Travel to the Riverside Drive exit. Go south on Riverside Drive to 122nd Street. From the south, follow the Henry Hudson Parkway to the Ninety-fifth Street exit. Go north on Riverside Drive to 122nd Street. A limited amount of street parking is available.

By subway: The 1 or 9 trains stop at the West 116th Street Station at Broadway. Walk six blocks north, and two blocks west.

By bus: The M5 route follows Riverside Drive to 122nd Street.

Stamping Locations and What the Cancellations Say
Grant Memorial Visitor Center information desk

☐ General Grant National Memorial/New York, NY ❿

32 Governors Island National Monument

see map on page 84
New York, New York
(212) 825–3045
www.nps.gov/gois

Number of cancellations: One

Difficulty: Tricky

About this site: If you're not looking in the right direction as you take the ferry from Battery Park to the Statue of Liberty, you'll probably miss Governors Island—but this unassuming little spot played a major role in the American Revolution, the War of 1812, the Civil War, and in peacetime military maneuvers.

Originally the home of the Lenape Indian tribe, the island came to General George Washington's attention as an important defensive point against the encroaching British, so he had earthworks constructed here. During the Battle of Brooklyn, the largest battle of the Revolution, the island's strategic position gave it strength as its artillery beat back the British forces. (Despite this heroic effort, the battle resulted in an eight-year occupation of New York City by the British.)

Used in the ensuing centuries as a prisoner of war camp, a military prison, a U.S. First Army headquarters, and a Coast Guard station, the island's historic structures finally became a national monument in 2001.

Stamping tips: The bookstore and visitor center are lodged in the first building to the left of the ferry dock. Obtain the cancellation from a ranger at the bookstore after your tour of the island.

It's critical to call Governors Island for the most current information on the ferry and the park's operating hours before visiting. Governors Island is a new national monument, and many changes are taking place on the island and within the park—so ferry departure points, opening and closing times, and public access are still in flux.

In 2007, the ferry to Governors Island departed from the Battery Maritime Building, located at 10 South Street at the corner of Whitehall and South Streets and next door to the Staten Island ferry terminal in lower Manhattan. The ferry ride is about ten minutes long. The Battery Maritime Building is not in Battery Park, and it is not the same location as the Statue of Liberty/Ellis Island ferry.

Public access to Governors Island during the summer season usually begins on the first Saturday in June, and runs through the first Saturday in September. The park is not open Sunday or Monday, and closes for July 4.

On Friday and Saturday, visitors can take a self-guided tour of Colonel's Row, the parade ground, and Fort Jay. During the week (Tuesday through Thursday), the one-and-a-half-hour ranger-guided tour is the only way to see the island, beginning with ferries departing from South Street at 10:00 A.M. and 1:00 P.M.

As there is no food service on the island except for a Saturday food cart, and running water and restroom facilities are very limited, the management recommends that you bring at least two quarts of water and a salty snack when you visit.

Don't miss this! After you've toured the super-fortified Castle Williams and Fort Jay—one of the most impressive star forts in the national park system—take some time to enjoy the landscaped grounds and historic homes beyond the national monument's boundaries. Much of the rest of Governors Island is a city and federal historic district, and it contains some splendid examples of period residential architecture.

Hours: The park is open from early June through early September (call for exact days). From Tuesday to Thursday, it is open for tours only, when 10:00 A.M. and 1:00 P.M. ferries dock. On Friday and Saturday, it is open from 10:00 A.M. to 5:00 P.M. The site is closed Sunday and Monday.

Fees: Admission to the park is free. Ferry tickets can be purchased online at nywatertaxi.com, or by calling (212) 742–1969.

How to get there: Automobiles are not permitted on Governors Island.

To reach the ferry by car from the East Side, take the FDR Drive south to exit 1 for the Battery Park/Staten Island ferry exit. From the West Side, take the West Side Highway/West Street to the FDR, and exit at South Street as you emerge from the Battery Park Tunnel.

The M1, M6, and M15 buses serve lower Manhattan near the Battery Maritime Building. The 4 and 5 subway lines at Bowling Green, the W and R lines at Whitehall/South Ferry, and the 1 train at South Ferry all provide access to the park.

Stamping Locations and What the Cancellations Say

Building 140–Bookstore and Visitor Contact Station
Governors Island

☐ Governors Island NM/New York, NY ⓞ

33 Hamilton Grange National Memorial

see map on page 84
New York, New York
(212) 825–6872
www.nps.gov/hagr

Number of cancellations: One

Difficulty: Challenging

About this site: This is the final home of Alexander Hamilton, co-author of the Federalist Papers and a critical player in developing the United States Constitution. As secretary of the treasury under President George Washington, Hamilton created the federal bank and worked to expand manufacturing throughout the first thirteen states. He ran for president but was never elected, and is probably most famous for the way he died—in a duel with then Vice President Aaron Burr, who blamed Hamilton, his former legal partner, for his own political losses.

Stamping tips: The site was closed during a move to its original location at Saint Nickolas Park, around the corner, scheduled for late 2007. There was discussion of moving the cancellation to General Grant National Memorial or to the Federal Hall National Monument in the interim, but a representative of the Manhattan Sites office tells me that the cancellation may be placed in storage until the site reopens. Be sure to call the Manhattan Sites office at (212) 825–6872 before you make the trip to Hamilton Grange, as this relocation had not occurred when this guide went to press.

❗ Don't miss this! The ranger-led tour of the upstairs rooms provides an up-close view of city living through the eyes of a key framer of our Constitution—a man who championed the cause of liberty both as a Revolutionary War aide-de-camp to General Washington, and as a lawmaker whose passion for freedom led him to shape the most fundamental rules of United States government. While the thirty-two-acre estate that surrounded the grange is long gone, the home reminds us that patriots came from the privileged class as well as from the rank and file—and all fought for the same cause, regardless of their background.

Hours: When it is open to the public, the site may be visited year-round, Wednesday through Sunday, from 9:00 A.M. to 5:00 P.M. It is closed on national holidays.

Fees: Admission to this park is free.

How to get there: The current site is at 287 Convent Avenue, at the intersection of 141st Street and Convent Avenue; the future location is in Saint Nickolas Park.

To reach the site by car, take Interstate 87 to exit 4 for East 149th Street. Go west on 149th Street across the bridge onto West 145th Street. Go west on 145th Street about 6 blocks to Convent Avenue. Go south 4 blocks on Convent Avenue to the site.

From the George Washington Bridge and Manhattan, follow Broadway to 141st Street. Go east on 141st Street to Convent Avenue.

The Seventh Avenue/Broadway 1 train stops at the West 137th Street Station on Broadway. From the station, go east to

Convent Avenue, then north to 141st Street. The A, B, C, and D trains stop at the West 145th Street Station on Saint Nickolas Avenue. From the train station, go west to Convent Avenue and south to 141st Street.

The Broadway M4 and M5 route is two blocks to the west of the site.

Stamping Locations and What the Cancellations Say

The Hamilton Home

287 Convent Avenue or Saint Nickolas Park

☐ Hamilton Grange National Memorial/New York, NY 🅞

34 Home of Franklin D. Roosevelt National Historic Site

Hyde Park, New York
(845) 229–9115 or (800) 337–8474
www.nps.gov/hofr

Number of cancellations: One

Difficulty: Easy

About this site: The long presidential career of Franklin Delano Roosevelt spanned three full terms and the first few months of a fourth, and Roosevelt's influence shaped many of the course-changing events of the twentieth century: rebuilding the American economy during and after the Great Depression; creation of the Civilian Conservation Corps, Social Security, the National Labor Board, and a dozen other programs through the New Deal he offered Americans; and America's entry into both the Pacific and the European theaters of the Second World War following the Japanese attack on Pearl Harbor.

To know Roosevelt's accomplishments is to know how our nation embraced a new model for government's ability to create a comfortable, safe way of life for its citizens. On the site of Springwood, his sumptuous home in Hyde Park, the mansion, a museum, and Roosevelt's presidential library present a comprehensive and satisfying overview of the life and work of one of our greatest presidents.

Stamping tips: This site reminds us that "easy" doesn't mean "stamp and run." With daily operating hours year-round, it's a snap to get the cancellation here—but there's a lot to see, so plan enough time (at least a couple of hours) to explore the museum, mansion, and grounds.

Tours often sell out early in the day during the spring, summer, and fall; call (800) 967–2283 for tour reservations. You can reserve your place on a tour up to five months in advance.

Don't miss this! If you don't know much about Roosevelt's career and accomplishments, spend time reviewing the well-presented displays in the museum. The sheer number of decisions, laws, and programs Roosevelt brought to fruition is impressive enough, but the fundamental changes he made in the way the United States views and protects its citizens continue to influence our lives today.

Add to this the opportunity to see the room from which Roosevelt broadcast his famous "fireside chats," the many accommodations made throughout his home for his disability, and the collection of mementos from his years in the White House, and you can begin to draw a complete picture of a man of wealth and privilege who never lost sight of the common people and their right to the pursuit of happiness.

Hours: The site is open year-round, seven days a week. Buildings are open from 9:00 A.M. to 5:00 P.M. The grounds are open from 7:00 A.M. to sunset. The site is closed Thanksgiving, Christmas, and New Year's Day.

Fees: $14.00 for adults for a two-day pass, including the guided tour of Springwood. The price also includes admission to the FDR Presidential Library and Museum, operated by the National Archives & Records Administration on the site. Free for children sixteen and under.

How to get there: From the New York State Thruway (Interstate 87), take exit 18 for New Paltz. Take New York 299 east to U.S. Highway 9W south, following signs to the Mid-Hudson Bridge. After the bridge crossing, follow overhead signs to northbound U.S. Highway 9. The park entrance is about 5 miles north on the left, at 4097 Albany Post Road in Hyde Park.

Stamping Locations and What the Cancellations Say

Bookstore in the Henry A. Wallace Visitor Center
(845) 229–5320

☐ Home of Franklin D. Roosevelt NHS/Hyde Park, NY **❶**

see map on page 84
New York State affiliated site
New York, New York
(212) 982–8420
www.nps.gov/loea

Number of cancellations: One

Difficulty: Easy

About this site: Millions of immigrants arrived in the United States in the late nineteenth and early twentieth centuries, many of them settling in New York's Lower East Side, where they adapted to the American way of life. The aging tenement building at 97 Orchard Street, down the street from the museum's visitor center, was home to thousands of transient families over the course of some seventy years—Irish, German, Jewish, Italian, Polish, and many other nationalities. The museum provides a vivid, often moving look back into the lives of our great-grandparents and their families through its rescued tenement apartments, each carefully refurbished to provide a realistic look at the living situations and daily existence of America's nine-teenth-century working class.

❶ Don't miss this! Take one or more of several different tours offered through the reconstructed apartments, which present the past in sharp contrast with the comfortable present. You'll visit the apartment of the Rogarshevsky family as it was in 1918—three rooms occupied by eight people—and the apartment-turned-garment shop run by Polish immigrants Harris and Jennie Levine. On the tour of the Sephardic-Jewish Confino family's ten-ement home, a costumed interpreter turns the tables and treats visitors as if they are the immigrants. You'll learn about the Sicil-ian family Baldizzi and the Gumpertz family from Germany, and the support systems these families discovered through *lands-manshafts,* associations of people with similar backgrounds. If your ancestors came through this neighborhood a hundred years ago, or through one of dozens of tenements like this in New York City and other coastal centers throughout the Northeast, you'll find treasures in the stories of strength and survival that fill this living museum's rooms.

Hours: The museum is open daily year-round; advance reservations are recommended for tours. Tours are available Tuesday through Friday from 1:00 P.M. to 4:45 P.M., and Saturday and Sunday from 11:00 A.M. to 5:00 P.M. The museum is closed Christmas, Thanksgiving, and New Year's Day.

Fees: Tours are $17.00 for adults, $13.00 for students and seniors. The Federal Lands Recreation Pass is not accepted.

How to get there: The visitor center is located at 108 Orchard Street in Manhattan, between Delancey and Broome Streets. Parking is very limited, so public transportation (bus or subway) is recommended. Take the B or D subway lines, and exit at Grand and Chrystie. Walk east for four blocks, then turn left at Orchard Street, and walk north two blocks. Alternately, take the F train to Delancey Street or the J, M, or Z trains to Essex Street, then walk two blocks west (away from the Williamsburg bridge) to Orchard Street. Turn left, the visitor center is on the corner.

Stamping Locations and What the Cancellations Say
Visitor center, at the front counter

☐ Lower East Side Tenement Museum NHS/New York, NY **Ⓤ**

36 Martin Van Buren National Historic Site

Kinderhook, New York
(518) 758–9689
www.nps.gov/mava

Number of cancellations: One

Difficulty: Tricky

About this site: Our eighth president earned the nickname "Little Magician" early in his political career because of his ability to get others to talk about their views without revealing his own. Martin Van Buren's history as an elder statesman, former secretary of state, and vice president under Andrew Jackson helped secure his bid for the presidency, but his first and only term in that office suffered from financial woes inherited from his predecessor. Two months after Van Buren took office, the spectacular failure of 900 banks across the country caused the Panic of 1837, resulting in the worst depression of the nineteenth century and costing Van Buren a second presidential term.

Nonetheless, Van Buren's flamboyant zest for life shows throughout Lindenwald, his thirty-six-room estate, which he purchased during his presidency and expanded to a 226-acre working farm.

Stamping tips: This site is open daily from mid-May to October 31. From November through early May, the site closes for the winter.

❶ **Don't miss this!** Learn about Van Buren's idiosyncrasies, his popularity as a target for media criticism—especially political cartoonists—and his role in originating the universal term "OK" by taking the ranger-guided tour of the mansion.

Hours: The site is open daily from mid-May to October 31 from 9:00 A.M. to 5:30 P.M. It is closed November through April.

Fees: $5.00 for adults; $12.00 for families (up to four adults and accompanying children fifteen and younger). Admission is good for seven days.

How to get there: The site is at 1013 Old Post Road in Kinderhook. From the north, east, and west, take Interstate 90 to exit 12 for U.S. Highway 9 to Hudson (from Boston the exit is B1). Follow US 9 south 4.5 miles to New York 9H. Bear right on NY 9H, and continue another 4.5 miles to the park on the right. (The site is on NY 9H, not US 9.)

Stamping Locations and What the Cancellations Say

Martin Van Buren National Historic Site Visitor Center

☐ Martin Van Buren National Historic Site/Kinderhook, NY ❶

37 North Country National Scenic Trail

New York NPS Affiliated Area
New York to North Dakota
(608) 441–5610
www.nps.gov/noco
Eastern time zone in New York (trail spans seven states)

Number of cancellations: Two in New York State, plus two additional cancellations at park sites

Difficulty: Tricky

About this site: Crossing a national park, ten national forests, many state and local forests and parks, and even some private land, this work-in-progress footpath will rival the Appalachian Trail in length when it's completed—and it already offers many excellent scenic hikes across seven states.

The final trail will stretch 4,600 miles, making it the longest continuous hiking trail in the United States. Currently, about 1,300 trail miles are officially completed, and many more segments are passable even while work on them continues. The trail begins in New York's Adirondack region and crosses Pennsylvania, Ohio, Michigan, Wisconsin, Minnesota, and North Dakota.

Stamping tips: If you're traveling during a transitional season and you're not sure if the Finger Lakes National Forest office, home of one of the cancellations, will be open that day, call ahead.

Don't miss this! The lengths of the North Country National Scenic Trail that pass through New York State provide both easy-to-moderate rambles through wooded countryside and old-growth forest, and challenging hikes through rugged terrain, with plenty of hills to get your heart pumping. You'll be rewarded with spectacular views of the Adirondacks, Catskills, and Bristol Hills, three ranges that traverse much of upstate New York, as well as vast green and gold expanses of farmland and wildlife-rich natural preserves. If you're looking for all that is beautiful in New York State—and an in-depth examination of what lies beyond Manhattan's skyscrapers and concrete—the North Country trail is an ideal way to find it.

Hours: The trail is open daily.

The Hector Ranger District office of the Finger Lakes National Forest is open in summer Monday through Friday from 8:00 A.M. to 4:30 P.M., and Saturday from 10:00 A.M. to 4:30 P.M. In winter, the office is open Monday through Friday from 8:00 A.M. to 4:30 P.M., and is closed on weekends.

Fort Stanwix Visitor Center is open daily year-round, from 9:00 A.M. to 5:00 P.M. It is closed Thanksgiving, Christmas, and New Year's Day.

Fees: Admission to trail segments is free.

How to get there: To reach the stamping location at Fort Stanwix National Monument, take the New York State Thruway (Interstate 90) to exit 32 (Westmoreland), and follow the signs to the monument. Fort Stanwix is at 112 E Park Street in Rome.

To reach the stamping location in the office of the Finger Lakes National Forest, take the New York State Thruway to exit 41. Turn south on New York 96A, and follow this to New York 414. Continue south on NY 414 into Hector (about 33 miles from Seneca Falls). The office is at 5218 NY 414 in Hector.

To hike the North Country National Scenic Trail, obtain maps from the North Country Trail Association at www.northcountry trail.org.

Stamping Locations and What the Cancellations Say

Fort Stanwix National Monument Bookstore
(315) 336–2090

☐ North Country National Scenic Trail/New York **Ⓓ**

☐ Erie Canalway NHC/Rome, NY **Ⓤ**

☐ Fort Stanwix National Monument/Rome, NY **Ⓤ**

Hector Ranger District Office of the Finger Lakes National Forest
5218 NY 414, Hector
(607) 546–4470

☐ North Country National Scenic Trail/New York **Ⓓ**

38 Sagamore Hill National Historic Site

Oyster Bay, New York
(516) 922–4788
www.nps.gov/sahi

Number of cancellations: Five

Difficulty: Easy

About this site: You're at the home of Theodore Roosevelt, one of the nation's most distinctive presidents—so interesting, in fact, that this is one of three national historic sites devoted to his memory in New York State alone. Roosevelt lived here from 1886 until his death in 1919, and he used this estate as the "Summer White House" during his two terms as the twenty-sixth president. He raised six children in this twenty-three-room Victorian mansion, ending his workday at 4:00 P.M. to spend time with his family—and meanwhile pursued his love of the arts, his passion for ornithology and all forms of nature, and wrote thirty-six books in the top-floor Gun Room.

Roosevelt's career in public service began well before his presidency, as he reformed the federal civil service and the New York City Police Department, winning acclaim for banning the sale of alcohol on Sundays. Roosevelt took the reins as governor of New York State in 1898, and rose to become vice president under William McKinley in 1901. McKinley's assassination later that year transformed the venerable TR into a president overnight, giving him the "bully pulpit" from which he enacted sweeping reforms and legislation.

Stamping tips: These cancellations are easy to get, but if you want to feel that you've earned the nature trail cancellation, be sure to walk the path that leads down to the Cold Spring Harbor beach most used by the Roosevelt family. Rangers lead nature walks along this trail on Sunday mornings in summer; at any other time, you can hike the moderately challenging trail on your own—but in spring and summer, bring insect repellant, as the mosquitoes can be relentless.

Don't miss this! While the cancellations at the Old Orchard museum are duplicates, this is the place to learn more about the life and work of one of our most fascinating presidents. Exhibits tell stories of TR's greatest accomplishments and the many challenges he encountered and overcame, while providing a glimpse of the good life at Sagamore Hill. You'll also discover more about Roosevelt's children and how they thrived in the shadow of their remarkable father.

Hours: In winter, the park is open Wednesday through Sunday, and closed Monday and Tuesday, Thanksgiving Day, Christmas Eve, Christmas, New Year's Eve, and New Year's Day. The Theodore Roosevelt home is open for tours from 10:00 A.M. to 4:00 P.M. The visitor center and bookstore are open from 9:00 A.M. to 4:45 P.M. The Old Orchard museum is open from 10:00 A.M. to 4:00 P.M.

Beginning on Memorial Day and continuing through Labor Day, the park and sites are open seven days a week. The grounds are open daily from dawn to dusk.

Fees: The park grounds can be visited without charge. First floor viewing may be offered at 4:20 P.M. for visitors who were unable to get an earlier tour, and is $3.00 for adults and free to children fifteen and under. The Roosevelt Home tour is $5.00 for adults and free to children fifteen and under.

How to get there: Take the Long Island Expressway to exit 41N (New York 106). Follow NY 106 north for 4 miles. Turn right on New York 25A, and go 2.5 miles to the third traffic light at Cove Road. Turn left, and continue for 1.7 miles. Turn right on Cove Neck Road, and go 1.5 miles to Sagamore Hill, at 20 Sagamore Hill Road in Oyster Bay.

Stamping Locations and What the Cancellations Say

Sagamore Hill Visitor Center

☐ Sagamore Hill National Historic Site/Oyster Bay, NY **Ⓤ**

☐ Sagamore Hill NHS/Roosevelt Museum at Old Orchard **Ⓓ**

☐ Sagamore Hill NHS/Sagamore Hill Nature Trail **Ⓓ**

Old Orchard Museum

☐ Sagamore Hill NHS/Roosevelt Museum at Old Orchard **Ⓓ**

☐ Sagamore Hill NHS/Sagamore Hill Nature Trail **Ⓓ**

39 Saint Paul's Church National Historic Site

Mount Vernon, New York
(914) 667–4116
www.nps.gov/sapa

Number of cancellations: One

Difficulty: Easy

About this site: Founded in 1665, this church represents one of America's oldest Christian parishes, one that played a role as a hospital in the American Revolution and became a center of military activity throughout that pivotal war. Remaining much as it was since its original construction, this little church preserves a 300-year-old cemetery and a bell that was cast at the same foundry as the Liberty Bell, as well as one of the oldest functioning organs in the country.

Stamping tips: This park is not open on weekends, except for special programs. If you want to visit on a weekend, call the park to see if programs or presentations are scheduled (and consider staying for the program once you have the cancellation, as such park programs usually feature historical information most of us would not discover on our own).

❶ Don't miss this! The museum and tour are far more charming than casual visitors might expect at first glance—especially if you take the guided tour provided by a park staff member. While you have your choice of three self-guided walking tours that feature the Revolutionary War activity at the church, the Civil War, or the colonial period, the ranger-led tour will give you an overview of all three, as well as a more focused examination of the cemetery and its history.

Hours: The church is open Monday through Friday, 9:00 A.M. to 5:00 P.M. It is closed weekends and national holidays.

Fees: Admission to the park is free.

How to get there: If traveling by car, take Interstate 95 to exit 13/Conner Street, which is in the northern Bronx. Turn onto Conner Street. This is a right if you've exited from I–95 south. If you exit from I–95 north, take a left at the first traffic light off the exit onto Tilloston Avenue, and then a left at the next light, onto Conner Street. Proceed north about 1 mile. Conner becomes Provost Street, and as you pass into Westchester County, it becomes South Third Avenue. After about 0.25 mile on South Third, make a right at the stop sign onto South Columbus Avenue. Turn right into the Saint Paul's Church driveway, which is just past the Salvation Army. The site is at 897 South Columbus Avenue in Mount Vernon.

By train: Take the Lexington Avenue IRT 5 Subway to Dyre Avenue Station in the Bronx. Service is provided seven days a week.

By bus: Route W55 operates half-hourly from the Dyre Avenue station to Saint Paul's Church.

Stamping Locations and What the Cancellations Say
Saint Paul's Church Visitor Center

☐ Manhattan Sites St. Paul's Church NHS/Mount Vernon, NY ❶

40 Saratoga National Historical Park

Stillwater, New York
(518) 664–9821
www.nps.gov/sara

Number of cancellations: Two, including a cancellation for Erie Canalway National Heritage Corridor

Difficulty: Easy

About this site: One of the most glorious colonial victories of the American Revolution took place here at Saratoga in battles on September 19 and October 7, 1777—battles that proved to be the undoing of British General John Burgoyne's plans for a quick victory. The month-long siege, during which Burgoyne waited in vain for reinforcements, finally ended in a muddy, bloody battle in which thousands of British soldiers lost their lives.

In the end, Burgoyne had no choice but to surrender to the Americans twenty-eight days after his first advance on Saratoga. The surrender heartened supporters of American Independence, and this turning point in the war is now regarded as one of the most decisive battles in world history.

Stamping tips: While the visitor center is open daily, the auto tour, Saratoga Monument, and Schuyler House are only open during the late spring, summer, and early fall. It's easy to get the cancellation at any time of year, but your visit will be more enjoyable if you arrive during the seasons when the other attractions are open.

Don't miss this! You can take the auto tour with nothing more than the park's official map and guide to read at each tour stop, but the 9-mile loop trail comes alive when you pop in the park's self-guiding cassette tape and listen to it as you drive. For a nominal fee, you can purchase the tape and keep it as a memento of your visit. The tape features period music and an easy-to-follow narrative describing the major players, troop movements, and military strategy of the battle.

Hours: The battlefield visitor center is open daily from 9:00 A.M. to 5:00 P.M. It is closed Thanksgiving, Christmas, and New Year's Day.

The tour road is usually open from April 1 to mid-November, depending upon weather conditions.

Schuyler House is open for guided tours Wednesday to Sunday, 9:30 A.M. to 4:30 P.M., from Memorial Day weekend through Labor Day.

Saratoga Monument is open Wednesday to Sunday, 9:30 A.M. to 4:30 P.M., from Memorial Day weekend through Labor Day.

Fees: $3.00 per person on foot, bike, or horse, good for seven days; $5.00 per vehicle, good for seven days.

How to get there: Saratoga National Historical Park is located 40 miles north of Albany, and 15 miles southeast of Saratoga Springs, at 648 New York 32.

From Montreal and points north, take Interstate 87 to exit 14, and follow New York 29 east to Schuylerville, where the Schuyler House (at the south end of town) and the Saratoga Monument (uphill on New York 338/Burgoyne Road) are located. At the T intersection with U.S. Highway 4, turn right. The battlefield entrance is 8 miles south on US 4.

From Albany and points south, follow I-87 to exit 12. Turn right off the exit; you will be on New York 67. After the first light, move into the left lane (turning lane). At the second light, turn left onto U.S. Highway 9 going north. Turn right on County Road 108, and take CR 108 to County Road 76. Turn right, and take CR 76 to its intersection with County Road 75. Turn left on CR 75, and go north to New York 423. Turn right, and take NY 423 to NY 32. Turn left, and follow the signs to the park entrance.

Stamping Locations and What the Cancellations Say

Saratoga National Historical Park Visitor Center

☐ Saratoga Nat'l Historical Park/Stillwater, NY **①**

☐ Erie Canalway NHC/Stillwater, NY **①**

41 Statue of Liberty National Monument and Ellis Island

see map on page 84
Liberty Island, New York, New York
(212) 363-3200
www.nps.gov/stli

Number of cancellations: Two

Difficulty: Easy

About this site: Arguably the most recognizable symbol of freedom and democracy in the world, the Statue of Liberty came to the United States in 1885 as a gift of friendship from France, and continues to be hailed as a marvel of engineering and artistic expression.

This 305-foot-high monument, designed by sculptor Frederic Auguste Bartholdi, underwent an extensive renovation that was completed in 1986, in time to celebrate the centennial of the statue's dedication. Visitors can enter the monument and look up through a glass ceiling to see the internal structure of the statue, and then continue to the pedestal observation deck to view the New York City skyline. Lady Liberty welcomes more than three million visitors each year.

About twelve million immigrants from virtually every country in Europe and beyond entered the United States from 1892 to 1954 through Ellis Island, the largest American gateway to the nation of freedom and opportunity. Today this formidable structure houses a fascinating museum with a wide array of permanent and changing exhibits, many of which are accessible to the hearing impaired.

Stamping tips: The official Passport cancellation for Ellis Island is at the information desk as you enter, not in the bookstore. While there are cancellations at each end of the bookstore, these are bonus cancellations with a picture of the Ellis Island building, not the official Passport cancellation. Be sure to ask for the cancellation you want at the information desk.

As the Statue of Liberty is a global icon, the U.S. government requires all visitors to go through a federal security screening process. You will have to pass through metal detectors to board the ferry, so leave your pocketknives, metal nail files, and other small, sharp objects in your hotel room or your car. Entry to the monument on Liberty Island requires a second screening.

Don't miss this! Take full advantage of all the opportunities to tour Liberty Island and the statue, and to enjoy the audio tour at Ellis Island. Plan to spend at least an hour or more at Liberty to stand in the shadow of this magnificent work of art, and consider how many people traveled thousands of miles at great personal peril to glimpse this statue and know that they would live, work, and raise their children in a free country.

You will need at least two hours at Ellis Island to truly understand the magnitude of the massive period of immigration of which it was an integral part, and its significance in changing the

American way of life through the work of these newcomers' hands and the vitality of their cultural backgrounds.

You can tour Ellis Island's three floors on your own, but the best way to grasp the events is by taking a ranger-guided tour or renting the audio tour. Through music, stories, and the voices of people who passed through the island's screening and examination procedures, the audio tour provides a manageable overview of the experience of entering America through its gangways and gates. A first visit to Ellis Island can be overwhelming, but the tours bring home the most important messages simply and with great entertainment value.

The American Family Immigration History Center is an exciting interactive program at the museum for the descendants of families who arrived at Ellis Island during the great immigration. You can access the passenger records of the ships that carried some twenty-two million immigrants, crew members, and other passengers to the Port of New York and Ellis Island. More than 100 million Americans may find records of their families' beginnings in the New World here. Highly skilled, well-informed experts on American genealogy are ready to help you find your ancestor's name in a ship's manifest using the center's powerful search engines, and to track other information that may be useful in learning more about your heritage. Check at www.ellisisland records.org to find out what records, documents, or other materials to bring with you to aid in your search.

Hours: The islands are open every day except Christmas. The Statue of Liberty and Ellis Island are open from 9:30 A.M. to 5:00 P.M.

To be sure that you'll get a seat on a ferry, purchase ferry tickets in advance or come early in the day. The last ferry leaves for the statue and Ellis Island at 4:30 P.M.; 3:15 P.M. in the off-season.

Fees: Admission to each park is free.

On Liberty Island, the National Park Service limits the number of visitors that can be inside the monument. "Time Pass" reservations are required to enter the monument. They are available free from the ferry company with the ticket purchase.

Ferry tickets cost $12.00 for adults, $10.00 for seniors (sixty-two and older), and $5.00 for children under twelve.

How to get there: Liberty and Ellis Islands are only accessible by ferry service. Statue Cruises, LLC, operates ferries from New York and New Jersey. One round-trip ferry ticket includes visits to both islands. For current ferry schedule information and advance ticket purchases, call (212) 269–5755 (for New York) or (201) 435–9499 (for New Jersey), or visit the Web site at www.statue cruises.com. You may also make reservations for tours of the statue at statuereservations.com.

The Statue Cruises ferry terminal in Manhattan is in Battery Park. From the east, take any bridge or tunnel to Manhattan. Take FDR Drive south to the last exit (exit 1). Take Broad Street to Water Street. Turn left on Water Street to Battery Park.

By bus, take the M1, M6, or M15 bus to Battery Park.

By subway, take the 1 train to South Ferry, 4 or 5 to Bowling Green, R or W train to Whitehall Street.

Stamping Locations and What the Cancellations Say

Visitor center on Liberty Island
(212) 363–3200
☐ Statue of Liberty N.M./New York, NY ⓤ

Information counter at Ellis Island
(212) 363–3200
☐ Ellis Island/N. J./N. Y. ⓤ

42 Theodore Roosevelt Birthplace National Historic Site

see map on page 84
New York, New York
(212) 260–1616
www.nps.gov/thrb
Number of cancellations: One
Difficulty: Tricky

About this site: Before moving to Sagamore Hill with his parents in 1885, Theodore Roosevelt—who would grow up to become the twenty-sixth president of the United States—lived at 20 East Twentieth Street in Manhattan. In this house, young "Teedie" overcame childhood weakness and chronic illnesses to establish what he would later call "the strenuous life": a daily regimen of challenging exercise that would lead to his hard-charging love of everything outdoors, from riding the North Dakota range to big-game hunting. During his presidency, Roosevelt established the U.S. Department of Forestry and championed programs for the conservation of public lands.

Five rooms of this reconstructed house (the original was demolished in 1916) have been decorated by Roosevelt's wife and sisters using many of the original furnishings, so they are much as they were during his childhood.

Stamping tips: The site is closed Sunday and Monday, and on all federal holidays. If you're spending the weekend stamping in New York, make this stop on Friday or Saturday.

❶ Don't miss this! You'll learn more about Teddy Roosevelt from the guided tour than you will on your own—tours are given every hour on the hour, and the rangers know their TR history and trivia. While Roosevelt clearly grew up as a child of privilege, the stories of his challenges with illness and his innovative, self-styled recovery plan reveal a great deal about the drive that made him worthy of a Nobel Peace Prize later in life—and then, worthy of inclusion on Mount Rushmore.

Hours: The site is open Tuesday through Saturday from 9:00 A.M. to 5:00 P.M. The last tour begins at 4:00 P.M. It is closed Sunday, Monday, and federal holidays.

Fees: $3.00 for adults; free for children seventeen and under.

How to get there: Driving and parking in Manhattan are not recommended.

By subway: The Lexington Avenue 6 train stops at the East Twenty-third Street station on Park Avenue South. Express 4 and 5 trains stop at Union Square. The N and R trains stop at the East Twenty-third Street station on Broadway.

By bus: Routes M6 and M7 on Broadway, route M1 on Park Avenue South, and route M23 cross-town on Twenty-Third Street all stop within close proximity to the site. Service operates seven days a week.

The site is at 20 East Twentieth Street, between Fifth Avenue and Park Avenue South, three blocks north and one block west of the northern end of Union Square.

Stamping Locations and What the Cancellations Say

Visitor center at Theodore Roosevelt Birthplace National Historic Site

☐ Theodore Roosevelt Birthplace NHS/New York, NY **❶**

43 Theodore Roosevelt Inaugural National Historic Site

Buffalo, New York
(716) 884–0095
www.nps.gov/thri

Number of cancellations: Two, including one for Erie Canalway National Heritage Corridor

Difficulty: Easy

About this site: In early September 1901, an assassin delivered a bullet to President William McKinley's abdomen while the president stood in a receiving line shaking hands with visitors to the 1901 Pan-American Exposition. When McKinley died eight days later, his vice president, Theodore Roosevelt, took the oath of office and became the twenty-sixth president of the United States in the home of Ansley Wilcox, a prominent Buffalo citizen. The Wilcox residence now serves as a museum, with several restored rooms of the Victorian period and a permanent exhibit room that tells the story of McKinley's death and Roosevelt's inauguration.

❶ Don't miss this! It's really worth studying the displays that tell the story of McKinley's assassination. Not only is the tale a stunning reminder of the miracles of modern medicine we enjoy today—advances that might have minimized the president's wound instead of forcing him to lay on his deathbed for days—it also serves as a dramatic example of why our nation's leaders now must travel with a constant circle of Secret Service bodyguards.

Hours: The site is open Monday to Friday from 9:00 A.M. to 5:00 P.M., and Saturday and Sunday from noon to 5:00 P.M. The last tour begins at 4:15 P.M.

Fees: $5.00 for adults, $3.00 for seniors (sixty-two and over) and students (fifteen to eighteen or with valid college identification), $1.00 for children six to fourteen, and free for children five and under. The family rate (for two parents/guardians and children) is $10.00.

How to get there: From the east, take Interstate 90 west to exit 51. Take exit onto New York 33 west (Kensington Expressway), and head into the downtown area. Continue west for 6.5 miles on NY 33. Take the Goodell Street exit, and get into the center lane of Goodell. Follow the signs to Delaware Avenue. At Main Street, continue to follow the signs to Delaware Avenue, veer left around Saint Louis Church, and go west on Edward Street. To reach the free parking lot, turn right at the first street, Franklin, and travel 2⅔ blocks north. The lot entrance is on the left. The park site is at 641 Delaware Avenue.

From the south or west, take I–90 to exit 53 for Interstate 190 north. Take I–190, and go west for 5.5 miles to exit 8 for Niagara Street. Turn left on Niagara Street and go northwest for 0.7 mile to Porter Avenue. Turn right onto Porter Avenue, and go northeast to Symphony Circle. Pass through Symphony Circle (Porter becomes North Street). Go east for 0.5 mile to Delaware Avenue. Turn right onto Delaware Avenue. The site is on your left.

Stamping Locations and What the Cancellations Say

Visitor center at Theodore Roosevelt Inaugural National Historic Site

☐ Theodore Roosevelt Inaugural NHS/Buffalo, NY ⓤ
☐ Erie Canalway NHC/Buffalo, NY ⓤ

44 Thomas Cole House National Historic Site

New York NPS Affiliated Site
Catskill, New York
(518) 943–7465
www.thomascole.org
Number of cancellations: One
Difficulty: Tricky
About this site: Even if you would never consider yourself an expert on fine art, you will recognize the distinctly American, universally appealing style of landscape painting that originated with Thomas Cole. The most famous founder of the Hudson River School of Art, Cole became a popular artist and public figure in his lifetime by capturing the lush, tranquil views of the Hudson

and the surrounding Catskill Mountains on canvas, displaying an extraordinary understanding of light and shadow and an uncanny ability to reproduce what he saw with accuracy and skill. At Cedar Grove, you can tour the studio where Cole created many of his most famous paintings, and see how he lived an artist's fantasy in these dreamlike surroundings.

Stamping tips: Hours are limited to weekends and summer/fall holidays, so plan your trip between May and October for your best chance at getting this cancellation.

Don't miss this! In addition to the house tour, Cedar Grove offers a Hudson River School Art Trail that takes you to many of the spots where Thomas Cole and his contemporaries painted their glorious landscapes. Pick up the full-color brochure at Cedar Grove, and then walk or drive (the total trail is 15 miles long) to see the views as artists Frederic Church, Asher B. Durand, Sanford Gifford, and Jasper Cropsey saw them in the 1800s—in fact, most of these landscapes are very much as they were nearly 200 years ago.

To see them all, you will need to leave your car and walk trails ranging from easy to strenuous—particularly to view Prospect Rock—but the panoramic view of the Hudson River valley, one seen by only the most motivated hikers and art history seekers, is more than worth the effort.

Hours: The park is open from the first Saturday in May through the last Sunday in October on Friday, Saturday, and Sunday from 10:00 A.M. to 4:00 P.M.

In addition, the house is open Memorial Day, Labor Day, Columbus Day, and Independence Day from 1:00 to 4:00 P.M.

Fees: Admission to the Main House and Old Studio is by guided tour only. The fee is $7.00 for adults, $5.00 for seniors and students with identification. Admission to the grounds is free of charge.

How to get there: The site is at 218 Spring Street in Catskill. From Interstate 87, take exit 21 for Catskill. Turn left at the stop sign, and then turn left onto New York 23 east. Go 2 miles, and turn right at the light onto Spring Street (New York 385). Cedar Grove is on the left (use the shared driveway with Temple Israel).

From points east, take the Massachusetts Turnpike to the New York State Thruway (Interstate 90 west) to exit 2B for the Taconic Parkway. Take Taconic Parkway south to NY 23 west.

Make a left at the first light at the intersection of NY 23 and NY 385 (Spring Street), and follow the directions above.

Stamping Locations and What the Cancellations Say

Thomas Cole House

☐ Thomas Cole National Historic Site/Catskill, NY ❶

45 Upper Delaware Scenic and Recreational River

Narrowsburg, New York, and Beach Lake, Pennsylvania
(570) 685–4871
www.nps.gov/upde

Number of cancellations: Four in New York, four more are in Pennsylvania

Difficulty: Tricky

About this site: The protected 73.4 miles of the Upper Delaware River offer opportunities for freshwater fishing, hunting, boating, canoeing, birding, and simply admiring the scenery, but these pristine waters represent much more than a great place to play.

This river supported human life as early at 15,000 B.C., facilitated timber rafting in the late 1700s—bringing pine and hemlock downstream for use in industry—and became an agricultural center in the nineteenth century. As New York's economy shifted from agrarian to industrial, the river played an important role in the Northeast's meteoric growth when its waters transported anthracite from Pennsylvania for fuel, and bluestone and other gravels to New York City for use in building roads.

Today the Upper Delaware supplies more than seventeen million people with drinking water—and nearly 500,000 come every year to enjoy outdoor sports on and around the river.

Stamping tips: While the Upper Delaware River is open for recreational activity every day of the year, the facilities at the park are only open on weekends from May to the end of September. Additionally, like all ranger stations in the national park system, the Barryville Ranger Station is not staffed daily, and rangers are often out in the field, so collecting the cancellations there can be particularly challenging. Call the station or park headquarters at

(570) 729–7134 before you drive to Barryville to see if a ranger is scheduled to be there when you arrive.

❗ **Don't miss this!** One of the challenges of visiting the scenic and recreational rivers in the national park system is in actually finding a way to experience the rivers themselves, especially if water sports are not your first vacation choice.

This river arches between the Catskill Mountains and the Appalachian Plateau, the entryway to Pennsylvania's eastern mountain range, and there are a number of good reasons why the National Park Service chose to preserve the corridor. It showcases thick, undisturbed hemlock forests; the state's highest concentration of nesting bald eagles; food supplies that attract hundreds of bird species during the spring and fall migration; coyotes, bobcats, and endangered river otters; and sparkling blue water rushing past mile after mile of gently curving mountains…it's worth packing a picnic, pulling out the binoculars, and stopping for much more than the cancellations.

Typically, you won't ride thrilling rapids on this river unless you arrive right after a heavy rain or the release of a tributary—the rapids are generally Class I and II—but scenic float trips are among the Upper Delaware's most popular attractions. Placid pools and a gentle current glide your raft through highland contours covered in green. Rent a canoe from one of the many liveries along the river, or schedule a fishing expedition with one of the area's experienced guides. Just be sure to dress appropriately for water sports, as the river never really warms up to a safe temperature, even in the heat of summer.

Hours: The Narrowsburg Information Center is open Memorial Day weekend to Labor Day weekend, Friday to Sunday from 9:30 A.M. to 4:30 P.M. It is open on September weekends from 9:30 A.M. to 4:30 P.M.

The Zane Grey Museum is open from Memorial Day weekend to Labor Day weekend, Friday to Sunday from 10:00 A.M. to 5:00 P.M. The last tour is at 4:30 P.M. From September to mid-October, it is open weekends from 10:00 A.M. to 5:00 P.M. (last tour at 4:30 P.M.). It is closed during the winter except for a special weekend open house the last weekend in January, in honor of Zane Grey's birthday.

Fees: Admission to this park is free.

How to get there: From New York City, take Interstate 87 (New York State Thruway) north to New York 17 north. Follow NY 17 to Interstate 84. Take I–84 east to Port Jervis (exit 1), then US 6 west to New York 97, and head north on NY 97. Narrowsburg is 30 miles north on NY 97.

From Albany, take I–87 (New York State Thruway) south to Kingston (exit 19), then follow US 209 south to NY 17 west, which leads to Monticello. From Monticello, take New York 17B to New York 52, and head west on NY 52. From the NY 52 junction with NY 97, head north to Narrowsburg.

Stamping Locations and What the Cancellations Say

Narrowsburg Information Center
Main Street, Narrowsburg
(570) 685–4871

☐ Upper Delaware S&RR/Beach Lake, PA Ⓓ

☐ Upper Delaware S&RR/Zane Grey Museum Ⓓ

Barryville Ranger Station
Barryville
(845) 557–0222
Located on NY 97 about 16 miles south of Narrowsburg

☐ Upper Delaware Scenic & Recreational River/Beach Lake, PA Ⓓ

☐ Upper Delaware Scenic & Recreational River/Zane Grey Museum Ⓓ

46 Vanderbilt Mansion National Historic Site

Hyde Park, New York
(845) 229–9115 or (800) 337–8747
www.nps.gov/vama

Number of cancellations: One

Difficulty: Easy

About this site: If you've ever wondered how the other one-hundredth-of-one-percent lived at the height of the Industrial Revolution, the Vanderbilt Mansion provides the voyeuristic glimpse we crave of the lives of the super-rich and famous. In this fifty-four-room mansion, Frederick Vanderbilt—railroad baron and the grandson of Cornelius "Commodore" Vanderbilt, the richest man of his generation—surrounded himself with the finest things in existence, leading the *New York Times* to call the 600-acre estate, "the finest place on the Hudson between New York and Albany." Frederick and his wife, Louise, maintained a staff of sixty domestics and filled the home with the luxurious furnishings and belongings you see today.

Don't miss this! Frederick Vanderbilt particularly loved the grounds of the estate, especially his woods—and you will as well, when you walk the gentle paths that curve through the trees along the Hudson River. If you're lucky enough to visit this site on a bright spring day, you'll see flowering trees in bloom around the sun-dappled trail, just as the richest man in America did when he strolled here with his wife and dog. After the conspicuous consumption inside the mansion, this natural scene is a refreshing reminder that there's more to life than huge piles of money—and, as most of us will never see the kind of wealth that typified the Vanderbilts, it's good to remember that our more normal lives have meaning of an entirely different kind.

Hours: The site is open daily from 9:00 A.M. to 5:00 P.M. It is closed Thanksgiving, Christmas, and New Year's Day. The grounds are open year-round from 7:00 A.M. until sunset.

Fees: $8.00 for adults for a guided tour of the first and second floors and basement. Children under fifteen are free.

How to get there: From Interstate 87, take exit 18 (New Paltz). Follow New York 299 east to U.S. Highway 9W south, following signs to the Mid-Hudson Bridge (also known as the Franklin Delano Roosevelt Bridge). After the bridge crossing, follow signs to U.S. Highway 9 north. The park entrance is in about 7 miles on the left.

Stamping Locations and What the Cancellations Say

Vanderbilt Mansion Visitor Center Bookstore
(845) 229–7770

☐ Vanderbilt Mansion NHS/Hyde Park, NY ❶

Seneca Falls, New York
(315) 568–2991; (315) 568–0024
www.nps.gov/wori

Number of cancellations: Three, including one for Erie Canalway National Heritage Corridor and one for the Underground Railroad

Difficulty: Easy

About this site: Feminists unite! The First Women's Rights Convention in American history took place here on July 19 and 20, 1848, led by Elizabeth Cady Stanton, a Seneca Falls housewife and the mother of three sons. When Stanton and 300 others met at the Wesleyan Methodist Chapel, they ratified a document now inscribed in a water wall of marble: the Declaration of Sentiments, based on the language of the Declaration of Independence but declaring for the first time in U.S. history that "all men and women are created equal."

The sixty-eight women and thirty-two men who signed this document demanded that women receive the fundamental freedoms afforded to men: to vote, hold elected office, earn a living, attend college, enter into legal contracts, and divorce an abusive husband—liberties women did not receive from the federal government until many decades later. Visitors can tour Stanton's home, the M'Clintock House where the Declaration of Sentiments was written, the Wesleyan chapel, and the interpretive displays in the visitor center.

Don't miss this! As an ardent feminist and a resident of upstate New York, I can't say enough about the importance of exploring this site—especially for young female students or working professionals who have no firsthand recollection of the days before women could demand equal consideration for jobs and equal pay with their male coworkers.

The visitor center's second floor provides perspective both on the nineteenth-century challenges faced by crusaders like Stanton, Mary Ann M'Clintock, and Susan B. Anthony (who lived 45 miles down the road in Rochester), while making the critical point that gender-based discrimination and inequality still exist now, especially in lower income brackets.

Just down the road at 76 Fall Street, the National Women's Hall of Fame is a worthwhile stop. Every other year, the hall of fame inducts some of the nation's most prominent and influential women—living and dead—in virtually every profession and walk of life, detailing each woman's accomplishments in a biographical display. You'll recognize most of the names: Madeleine Albright, Hillary Rodham Clinton, Abigail Adams, Louisa May Alcott, Margaret Mead, Lucretia Mott, Sacagawea, and hundreds more.

Hours: The park is open daily from 9:00 A.M. to 5:00 P.M., except for Thanksgiving Day and all federal holidays during the winter months.

Fees: Admission to the park is free.

How to get there: From the New York State Thruway (Interstate 90), take exit 41 for New York 414. Turn right onto NY 414 after exiting the tolls. Follow NY 414 for approximately 4 miles. At the intersections of NY 414 and New York 5/U.S. Highway 20 (the same road at this point), turn left onto NY 5/US 20. Follow this road approximately 1.5 miles into the village of Seneca Falls. The visitor center is on the left at 136 Fall Street.

Stamping Locations and What the Cancellations Say

Women's Rights Visitor Center

☐ Women's Rights Nat'l Historical Park/Seneca Falls, NY ⓤ

☐ Erie Canalway NHC/Seneca Falls, NY ⓤ

☐ Women's Rights NHP/Underground RR Freedom Network ⓤ

Rhode Island

48 John H. Chafee Blackstone River Valley National Heritage Corridor

Rhode Island NPS Affiliated Area
Woonsocket, Rhode Island
(401) 762–0250
www.nps.gov/blac

Number of cancellations: Four, plus a cancellation for Roger Williams National Memorial. One more cancellation is available in Massachusetts.

Difficulty: Easy

About this site: Covering 400,000 acres and stretching from the Blackstone River in Worcester, Massachusetts, to Narragansett Bay in Providence, Rhode Island, this heritage corridor commemorates the influence of the Blackstone River's water power—generated by a 438-foot drop in altitude over 46 miles—on the growth of industry in this region. The first water-driven cotton-spinning factory, built by Sam Slater, harnessed the power of the river and set off a rush of mill construction that turned this area into a booming industrial landscape.

Stamping tips: While most of the stamping locations are open daily, the Corridor Commission Office in Woonsocket keeps weekday business hours, so plan to stop on Friday if you're making a weekend tour of this national heritage corridor.

It's up to you whether or not you collect all of the duplicate cancellations for the heritage corridor—your trip to Roger Williams National Memorial will net you the Blackstone River Valley cancellation as well as the national memorial cancellation—but if you do choose to pursue them all, the most efficient path would be to travel straight down Rhode Island 146 from Woonsocket to Pawtucket to Providence, making the side trip into Pawtucket on Rhode Island 15.

One duplicate cancellation is available in Massachusetts; see that chapter in this guide for more information.

❶ Don't miss this! Don't leave the Blackstone River valley without absorbing at least a little information about the lives of those who made the transition to wage labor in the area's mills and factories. Slater Mill and the Museum of Work and Culture both provide realistic portrayals of the quality of life people accepted when they chose the industrial way's long hours and regular pay, leaving the agricultural economy behind. Woonsocket's museum focuses on the French Canadian immigrants who populated this town, while Slater Mill features costumed interpreters who describe and demonstrate the textile mill workers' way of life, working conditions, and the tools they used to create products before electricity replaced many mechanical functions.

Hours: The Museum of Work and Culture is open Monday to Friday from 9:30 A.M. to 4:00 P.M., Saturday from 10:00 A.M. to 5:00 P.M., and Sunday from 1:00 to 4:00 P.M.

The Corridor Commission Office is open Monday to Friday from 8:00 A.M. to 5:00 P.M.; it is closed weekends.

The Blackstone Valley Visitor Center is open daily from 9:00 A.M. to 5:00 P.M.

The Roger Williams National Memorial is open daily from 9:00 A.M. to 4:30 P.M.; it is closed Thanksgiving, Christmas, and New Year's Day.

Fees: There are no admission fees to the corridor or to most of its regular programs.

The Museum of Work and Culture charges $6.00 for adults, $4.00 for seniors/students, and is free for children nine and under.

How to get there: RI 146 is the main highway running north and south between Providence and Worcester, with major intersections with Interstate 95 and Interstate 295. The Blackstone River valley is bordered on the east by Interstate 495 and on the west by Interstate 395. Directional signage points the way to visitor information centers.

Visitors traveling north from Providence on I–95 can take exit 27 or 28 for the Blackstone Valley Visitor Center in Pawtucket at 175 Main Street.

To reach the Roger Williams National Memorial, from I–95, take downtown exit 22A. Turn left at the first light onto Francis Street; continue to the next traffic light (the state house is right in front of you). Turn right onto Gaspee Street; turn right at the next light onto Smith Street; turn right at the next light onto Canal Street. Cross the three traffic lanes on Canal Street, and turn left into the memorial parking lot. The site is at 282 North Main Street.

To reach the sites in Woonsocket from Providence, take RI 146 north to Rhode Island 146-A (Eddie Dowling Highway). Continue to Providence Street, and turn right. Take Providence Street to South Main Street; turn right on South Main. The Museum of Work and Culture is at 42 South Main Street.

To reach the Corridor Commission Office, continue west on South Main to High Street (Rhode Island 122), and turn left, then take RI 122 to Depot Square.

Stamping Locations and What the Cancellations Say

Corridor Commission Office
1 Depot Square, Woonsocket
(401) 762–0250

☐ Blackstone River Valley Nat'l Heritage Corridor/Massachusetts & Rhode Island ①

Museum of Work and Culture
Market Square, 42 South Main Street, Woonsocket
(401) 769–WORK (9675)

☐ Blackstone River Valley Nat'l Heritage Corridor/Massachusetts & Rhode Island ①

Blackstone Valley Visitor Center
175 Main Street, Pawtucket
(800) 454–BVTC (2882) or (401) 724–2200

☐ Blackstone River Valley Nat'l Heritage Corridor/Massachusetts & Rhode Island ①

Roger Williams National Memorial Visitor Center
282 North Main Street, Providence
(401) 521–7266

☐ Blackstone River Valley Nat'l Heritage Corridor/Massachusetts & Rhode Island ①

☐ Roger Williams National Memorial/Providence, RI ①

49 Roger Williams National Memorial

Providence, Rhode Island
(401) 521–7266
www.nps.gov/rowi

Number of cancellations: Two, including one for the John H. Chafee Blackstone River Valley National Heritage Corridor

Difficulty: Easy

About this site: You may not know that our freedom of religion, one of the nation's fundamental rights, did not come into practice on the day the Pilgrims landed, but actually grew from the work of Anglican minister Roger Williams. Banished from Massachusetts for rejecting the Puritans' restrictive, controlling view of worship, Williams founded the colony of Providence in 1636 and established a haven for people from all religious belief systems, where they could live without interference from the government. Within two years, he co-founded the first Baptist church in the New World. Soon religious dissenters of all faiths came to Rhode Island and founded their own towns, making this cluster of colonies—and eventually, this tiny state—a bastion for free thought and the examination of many philosophies.

Don't miss this! The visitor center and memorial take only a short time to enjoy, but you may add a half-hour to walk the grounds and see some of the related sites in the neighborhood. The Hahn Memorial, a symbolic well on the park's 4.5-acre grounds, is named for the first Jewish citizen of Providence to hold elected office. On Prospect Terrace, a statue of Williams stands on the spot to which his and his wife's remains were moved in 1939; there's also a great view of the city from the terrace. Nearby, at 75 North Main Street, the First Baptist Meeting House hosts the congregation Williams founded in 1638—this picturesque chapel was built in 1775.

Hours: The park is open daily from 9:00 A.M. to 4:30 P.M.; it is closed Thanksgiving, Christmas Day, and New Year's Day.

Fees: Admission to the memorial is free.

How to get there: From Interstate 95 south, take downtown exit 22A. Turn left at the first light onto Francis Street; continue to the next traffic light (the state house is right in front of you). Turn right onto Gaspee Street; turn right at the next light onto Smith Street; turn right at the next light onto Canal Street. Cross the three traffic lanes on Canal Street, and turn left into the memorial parking lot. The site is at 282 North Main Street.

From I–95 north, take exit 23/State Offices. At the second light, turn left onto Smith Street. At the third light, turn right onto Charles Street, then left into the memorial parking lot.

Stamping Locations and What the Cancellations Say
Roger Williams National Memorial Visitor Center

☐ Roger Williams National Memorial/Providence, RI **❶**

☐ Blackstone River Valley Nat'l Heritage Corridor/Massachusetts & Rhode Island **❶**

50 Touro Synagogue National Historic Site

Rhode Island NPS Affiliated Site
Newport, Rhode Island
(401) 847–4794
www.nps.gov/tosy or tourosynagogue.org
Number of cancellations: One
Difficulty: Tricky
About this site: The very first Jewish house of worship built in the United States, Touro Synagogue opened during Hanukkah (celebrated in December) in 1763 and has functioned as a working synagogue ever since, except for a short period in the Revolutionary War when it served as a military hospital during the British occupation of Newport.

Newport became a safe haven for a growing American Jewish population because of the work of Roger Williams, John Clarke, William Coddington, and Ann Hutchinson, crusaders for freedom of religion, who founded Rhode Island as a place where all religions could thrive. Not only is this synagogue remarkable for its history, its architectural features reflect the strong influence of the Sephardic Jewish tradition that came to America from Spain and Portugal. Today an Orthodox Jewish congregation holds its worship services here.

Stamping tips: Take careful note of the limited hours here. The Jewish Sabbath begins Friday night at sundown and continues through Saturday night, so while Touro is open for worship at that time, no tours are given—and in strict observance of Jewish law, the bookstore is closed. The synagogue is also closed to tours on all Jewish holidays.

Don't miss this! The tour provides a brief but excellent overview of Jewish life in colonial America, as well as all the information you need about the architectural elements inside the sanctuary and their symbolic meanings. Here's a suggestion for an entirely different kind of experience: If you happen to be Jewish and it happens to be Friday night or Saturday morning, consider attending shabbat services with the Congregation Jeshuat Israel. The Orthodox Sephardic service is entirely in Hebrew and is practiced in the strictest Jewish tradition, so women sit upstairs in the gallery, while men sit below in the sanctuary. If you come from a less observant Jewish upbringing, you might find this fascinating, or at least culturally significant. In any case, you'll attend a service at the oldest synagogue in America, which may prove to be both meaningful and moving.

Hours: Hours vary by season. Visit the site's Web site before your trip, or call (410) 847–4794 for more information.

No tours are given on Saturdays or Jewish holidays. Additional hours may be scheduled during holiday weeks.

Fees: The tour costs $5.00 for adults and is free for children twelve and under.

How to get there: Touro Synagogue is located in downtown Newport at 85 Touro Street, close to Washington Square and the intersection of Spring and Touro Streets.

Stamping Locations and What the Cancellations Say

Touro Synagogue Foundation Bookstore

Located on the synagogue property

☐ Touro Synagogue NHS/Newport, RI ❶

Vermont

51 Marsh-Billings-Rockefeller National Historical Park

Woodstock, Vermont
(802) 457–3368
www.nps.gov/mabi

Number of cancellations: Two

Difficulty: Easy

About this site: Pay attention, because this gets complicated: When George Perkins Marsh was born on this farm in 1801, clear-cutting of Vermont's forests had nearly destroyed the land by allowing erosion to wash away the ground's nutrients, turning the landscape into a barren wasteland. Marsh, an attorney and self-styled conservationist, saw the destruction taking place around him and introduced the concept of land stewardship to America, focusing attention on the need for immediate action in his groundbreaking book, *Man and Nature,* printed in 1864.

Frederick Billings bought the property in 1869 and established a herd of scientifically managed Jersey cows, creating a model for farmers throughout Vermont and beyond to practice on their own. Billings used the recommendations in Marsh's book to reforest Woodstock and the surrounding area.

Billings's granddaughter, Mary French, married Laurance Spelman Rockefeller and inherited the property in the 1950s, modernizing it and establishing the Billings Farm Museum. Today this unit is the only national park site that interprets the history of conservation stewardship.

Don't miss this! Ranger-led tours of the Marsh-Billings-Rockefeller mansion and gardens take place hourly, but they are well worth the wait. Expert in their understanding of the conservation issues Marsh and Billings faced, the rangers paint the verbal picture of a denuded Vermont, making us more than grateful that we can no longer see that brutalized landscape for ourselves.

The mansion contains many paintings by artists of the Hudson River School, a movement that defined American art as separate and distinct from its European predecessors. These landscapes, many of which interpret the artist's vision with near-photographic realism, inspired a sense of admiration for both the sweeping vistas and the intimate nooks and crannies of New England's quiet countryside.

Finally, thousands of leaf-peepers visit this park and many others in Vermont to take in the brilliant reds and golds of autumn. The park's carriage roads and hiking trails are particularly well suited for a quiet walk through this magnificent natural show.

Hours: From April 30 to October 31, the Billings Farm & Museum is open daily from 10:00 A.M. to 5:00 P.M.

The carriage roads and trails are open year-round. The visitor center is open Memorial Day weekend to October 31 from 10:00 A.M. to 5:00 P.M. daily.

Fees: The mansion and gardens may be viewed by guided tour only. Adults cost $8.00, $4.00 for seniors, and children (under sixteen) are free.

Admission to the Billings Farm & Museum is $9.50 for adults, $8.50 for seniors over 65, $7.50 for students thirteen to seventeen, $5.00 for children five to twelve, and $2.50 for children three to four.

How to get there: From Interstate 89, take exit 1 to Woodstock/Quechee. Turn left on Vermont 4, and follow VT 4 for about 10 miles into Woodstock and the junction with Vermont 12 north. The park is about half a mile outside of town on VT 12, at 54 Elm Street in Woodstock. Parking is at the Billings Farm & Museum.

Stamping Locations and What the Cancellations Say

Billings Farm visitor center
Located at the desk

☐ Marsh-Billings-Rockefeller NHP/Woodstock, VT ●

Carriage Barn visitor center
Located at the desk

☐ Marsh-Billings-Rockefeller NHP/Woodstock, VT ●

About the Author

Randi Minetor has visited more than 200 national parks, and has written several books for FalconGuides, including the *Passport To Your National Parks® Companion Guides* series and two *National Park Pocket Guides*. Randi served as a consultant and writer for Eastern National's *Passport Explorer,* the big brother to the best-selling *Passport To Your National Parks®* book. Her groundbreaking book *Breadwinner Wives and the Men They Marry* (New Horizon Press, 2002) continues to receive national media  attention, and her articles have appeared in dozens of trade magazines on subjects ranging from municipal water system management to technical theater. She and her husband, Nic, live in Rochester, New York.